Adam Temple is a barrister at 3 Verulam Buildings, specialising in financial services law. He regularly appears for the Financial Conduct Authority in regulatory cases, and for banks, IFAs and insurance companies in all manner of disputes. He has particular expertise in FOS claims and is regularly instructed to advise on matters of systemic interest to his clients, including in judicial reviews of FOS decisions.

Devon Airey is a barrister at 3 Verulam Buildings with experience acting on banking and financial services disputes. She has assisted with cases arising from FOS decisions, as well as disputes under the Financial Services and Markets Act and the FCA Handbook.

A Practical Guide to Financial Ombudsman Service Claims

Second Edition

A Practical Guide to Financial Ombudsman Service Claims

Second Edition

Adam Temple
MA, BCL (Oxon)
Barrister, 3 Verulam Buildings

Devon Airey
BA (Cantab)
Barrister, 3 Verulam Buildings

Law Brief Publishing

Published 2025 by Law Brief Publishing, an imprint of Law Brief Publishing Ltd
30 The Parks
Minehead
Somerset
TA24 8BT

www.lawbriefpublishing.com

Paperback: 978-1-916698-84-0

PREFACE

The aim of this book is to provide a high-level guide to disputes before the Financial Ombudsman Service (or 'FOS'). We also look at how FOS decisions interact with litigation and how to challenge FOS decisions when unhappy with them.

One of the most important parts of financial services regulation is a guarantee that the clients of those who provide such services are able to complain and seek redress. For many such clients, the FOS represents an efficient and cost-effective means enabling them to do just that. In those cases which are not finally resolved by the FOS, the FOS proceedings will often represent the first step in a lengthier dispute which may not be resolved until a court finally gives judgment.

Whilst many FOS claims will not involve lawyers, our experience is that legal advisors often assist parties before the FOS (particularly on the respondent side, given their size or the availability of indemnity insurance). It seemed to us that, in light of this, there might be some use for a short book outlining the key parts of FOS procedure.

Given its complexity, we have not attempted to go into the full detail of the FCA Handbook's DISP chapter. Instead, we have tried to write what we hope is a helpful guide which will either enable the reader to find the answer to the main points about how FOS claims work, or at least be pointed in the right direction for more niche issues.

Anyone familiar with financial services regulation will know how frequently the regulator likes to update its rules. With that in mind, we have tried to state the law as at 7 November 2024, save that we managed to update references to the FCA and FOS's Memorandum of Understanding to refer to the updated version produced on 15 November 2024.

On 14 November 2024, the Chancellor of the Exchequer gave her Mansion House speech, including the suggestion that reform of the FOS is needed. This led to joint a 'Call for Input' from the FOS and the FCA, seeking views on reforms. Also, on 19 November 2024, the FOS confirmed that it would seek to charge claims management companies for pursuing complaints before the FOS (as discussed in Chapter 12), subject to parliamentary scrutiny and legislative approval. Such developments will be included in any future edition of this book.

Adam Temple
Devon Airey
November 2024

CONTENTS

TABLE OF ABBREVIATIONS AND COMMONLY USED TERMS

This book uses a number of abbreviations throughout, as set out below:

DISP	The 'Dispute Resolution: Complaints' section of the Financial Conduct Authority's Handbook
CRD	Capital Requirements Directive
CBTL	Consumer buy-to-let
FCA	Financial Conduct Authority
FOS	Financial Ombudsman Service
FSA	Financial Services Authority (the previous name of the Financial Conduct Authority)
FSMA	Financial Services and Markets Act 2000
Glossary	Glossary of the Financial Conduct Authority's Handbook
Handbook	The Rules and Guidance promulgated by the Financial Conduct Authority.
MiFID	Markets in Financial Instruments Directive
RAO	Financial Services and Markets Act 2000 (Regulated Activities) Order 2001

TABLE OF CASES

TABLE OF LEGISLATION

TABLE OF FCA HANDBOOK PROVISIONS

CHAPTER ONE

INTRODUCTION TO THE FOS

This book is about the Financial Ombudsman Service (or 'FOS'). The FOS is a key form of alternative dispute resolution for customers of financial institutions. It provides an important way of resolving a wide variety of claims and complaints.

The purpose of this book is to look at the principal issues that arise when the FOS is asked to determine a complaint. It also considers how the FOS relates to other dispute resolution procedures, most notably litigation.

The history of the FOS

While the concept of an ombudsman is long-standing in Scandinavian countries,[1] it was not until the Parliamentary Commissioner Act 1967 that the institution first made its way to Britain. The purpose of that commission was to provide a method of investigating and remedying complaints about central government that were brought through members of the House of Commons. Over time, its role expanded. Complaints can now be brought by members of the public, and it is today called the Parliamentary and Health Service Ombudsman. It allows complaints to be made against a wide array of government departments and services, as well as the NHS.

Since the first ombudsman in 1967, a number of ombudsmen have sprung up to regulate other industries. Many – such as the Legal Services Ombudsman and the Housing Ombudsman – have statutory bases. Others are purely voluntary.

---

1 Sweden's Parliamentary Ombudsman, for example, was formed in 1809.

The FOS falls into the former category though, as will be seen, many organisations sign up to its so-called 'voluntary jurisdiction' and would otherwise fall outside the scope of its mandatory powers. The FOS's legal basis comes from the Financial Services and Markets Act 2000 ('FSMA'). That legislation updated the existing law of financial regulation. It created the Financial Services Authority ('FSA') to oversee regulation. In 2012, the FSA was renamed the Financial Conduct Authority ('FCA').

FSMA created the FOS and in so doing brought together a wide array of existing ombudsmen (including the Insurance Ombudsman and Banking Ombudsman). Until 1 December 2001, the FOS applied the rules of the scheme under which the complaint would previously have been brought. For example, complaints formerly covered by the Banking Ombudsman would be considered against the rules of the Banking Ombudsman scheme. Since that date, the FOS has applied the provisions in the FCA's Handbook, as set out below.

The FCA Handbook: DISP

The FOS's rules and procedures are set out in the FCA Handbook. Specifically, they are contained in the chapter called 'Dispute Resolution: Complaints' (or 'DISP', as it is known).

The FCA Handbook is made under the FCA's powers pursuant to FSMA. It is divided into a series of sections. Its scope is wide, covering everything from identifying who falls within the scope of regulation, to the standards and duties with which they must comply, and what happens when things go wrong. It is this last issue – what happens when things go wrong – where the FOS comes in.

DISP is the part of the Handbook that deals with complaints brought against respondents before the FOS.[2] It contains both 'Rules' and 'Guidance'. The former are denoted by the presence of an 'R' after the relevant provision (e.g. '1.1.1R'). The latter are denoted with a 'G'. Rules create binding obligations on those who provide financial services in the

---

2 See the Introduction to DISP.

UK.[3] Guidance is not binding in the same way. Instead, it sets out explanations, information as to what may be needed in order to ensure compliance and recommended (but not mandatory) conduct.

The FCA Handbook: Glossary

Many words within the FCA Handbook are defined terms: all such defined terms are italicised in the text and, when viewed online, can be clicked to show the definition. When considering FCA Rules and Guidance it is important to consider such definitions.

How the FOS is set up

The FOS is a corporate body (a limited company) known as the Financial Ombudsman Service Limited. It is the 'scheme operator' required by s.225 of FSMA to oversee and run the ombudsman service. At the head of the FOS is a chairman and the board, whose members are directors of the FOS. Each director is appointed and liable to be removed from office by the FCA.[4]

Complaints are determined by a series of ombudsmen and adjudicators. FSMA makes provision for a Chief Ombudsman,[5] who is responsible for leading the panel of ombudsmen. Both the FOS and the Chief Ombudsman are required to submit a report each year to the FCA on the discharge of their functions.[6] The FOS is also required to produce annual budgets and plans.[7]

Each of the documents that the FOS is required to produce can be found

3 Those providing financial services in the UK are also referred to in this book as 'firms'.

4 FSMA, Schedule 17, Part II, paragraph 3.

5 FSMA, Schedule 17, Part II, paragraph 5.

6 FSMA, Schedule 17, Part II, paragraph 7.

7 FSMA, Schedule 17, Part II, paragraphs 9 and 9A.

on its website.

Sources of information

The FOS website[8] contains a host of information. Much is aimed at complainants, who are generally acting 'in person' (i.e. without lawyers).

Ombudsman News is a regular publication from the FOS discussing contemporary issues facing the FOS. Each issue also includes case studies on a particular topic, giving guidance to how the FOS reached its decisions in particular complaints. Recent editions have considered complaints arising out of authorised push payment ('APP') scams[9] or travel insurance in the wake of the COVID-19 pandemic.[10]

When considering whether the FOS complied with the rule of law, the Court of Appeal in *R (Heather Moor & Edgecomb) v FOS* [2008] EWCA Civ 642 referred to concerns that decisions were not (at that time) published by the FOS.[11]

However, since 1 April 2013, the FOS has published the final decisions of ombudsmen on its website. It is therefore possible to see the approach taken by the FOS in previous cases, which may assist in understanding what the FOS is likely to think 'fair and reasonable' (the standard the FOS applies when determining a dispute: see Chapter 11) in particular circumstances. FOS decisions are not formal precedents in the way that court decisions are, and the FOS is not bound by previous decisions when determining complaints. However, if a party wants to argue for a particular result, it can be useful to show how very similar facts have been dealt with previously.

The FOS also sometimes publishes anonymised provisional decisions, in areas where it is seeing multiple complaints. So, in October 2012, the

---

8 http://www.financial-ombudsman.org.uk.

9 Ombudsman News, Issue 194 (5 September 2024).

10 Ombudsman News, Issue 183 (10 August 2023).

11 See [85].

FOS started to see an upswing in complaints relating to interest rate hedging products and it decided to issue two provisional decisions on typical facts, setting out its approach. Final decisions on the same facts were then published in July 2013 (still anonymised).

Likewise, in the context of fractional ownership timeshares, the FOS issued final decisions on two lead cases, which were the subject of detailed consideration and industry submissions.[12]

The FOS also publishes 'case studies' on its website, which are broadly based on real-life cases, and are intended to reflect the FOS's view of common fact patterns.

The FOS as a source of new law

There have been occasions on which the FOS's approach to determining complaints has not only differed from the law as applied by the courts (see Chapter 11[13]), but where the law has subsequently followed the FOS's approach. In particular, there had been longstanding criticisms of English law's approach to minor non-disclosures when applying for insurance policies, and breaches of warranties within insurance policies. The FOS led the way in adopting a more flexible approach than that used in the courts, and that approach subsequently found its way into the Consumer Insurance (Disclosure and Representations) Act 2012 and the Insurance Act 2015.

The relationship between the FOS and the FCA

The relationship between the FOS and the FCA is principally set out in Schedule 17, part II of FSMA. The FOS is operationally independent of the FCA. However, the FCA has an interest in ensuring the FOS operates effectively as part of the FCA's 'consumer protection' objective.

---

12 See *R (Shawbrook) v FOS* [2023] EWHC 1069 (Admin) at [5].

13 In particular, the discussion contained there on *Options UK Personal Pensions LLP v Financial Ombudsman Service* [2024] EWCA Civ 541.

Therefore, paragraphs 2 and 3A of that Schedule imposes a series of basic duties on the FCA. They include, amongst other things:

1. A duty to take such steps as are necessary to ensure the FOS is capable of exercising its functions.

2. Making rules defining the FOS's compulsory jurisdiction.

3. Making rules defining the FOS's voluntary jurisdiction.

4. Specifying the maximum amount which the FOS is able to award as compensation.

5. Approving rules made by the FOS determining how costs of complaints are to be allocated.

6. Appointing and removing members of the FOS's board.

Further detail as to the relationship between the FOS and FCA can be found in a memorandum of understanding entered into between them in November 2024.[14] The purpose of that memorandum is to describe how the two bodies are to cooperate with each other in performing their functions under paragraphs 2 and 3A of Schedule 17 of FSMA. The memorandum was required to be executed pursuant to paragraph 3A(2) of that Schedule.

The memorandum sets out that, whilst it is the FCA's duty as regulator to ensure that its relevant markets function well, it is the FOS's duty to operate a scheme under which disputes can be heard. According to the memorandum, the purpose of the FOS is to enable disputes to be resolved quickly and with minimum formality.[15]

The memorandum also sets out the way in which the FOS's governance is to be handled.[16] This provides further guidance as to how the FCA is to exercise its functions over things such as reviewing the FOS's budgets

---

14 https://www.fca.org.uk/publication/mou/mou-fos.pdf.

15 See paragraph 13.

16 Paragraphs 20 - 22.

and reports, and appointing the FOS's directors. Paragraph 23 of the memorandum provides details of how the FOS and FCA are to cooperate so as to ensure that their approaches are '*complementary and consistent*'. There is also an agreement for the FOS and FCA to disclose information to one another for the purposes of them helping to discharge their functions.[17]

The FCA and FOS are also members of the 'regulatory family' that operates under the 'Wider Implications Framework'. The framework has Terms of Reference,[18] which explain that it is intended to assist various financial regulatory bodies to '*discuss openly, frankly and promptly issues that may have significant implications*' and to agree on appropriate action to take. The FCA publishes examples of its work, six-monthly 'issues logs' and annual reports from the Framework, on its website.[19]

The relationship between the FOS and the FCA has also developed through the FCA's introduction of the consumer duty. The effect of the FCA's consumer duty on the FOS and complaints handling is considered further in Chapter 20.

17 Paragraphs 26–30.

18 https://www.fca.org.uk/publication/corporate/wider-implications-framework-tor.pdf

19 https://www.fca.org.uk/about/wider-implications-framework

CHAPTER TWO

THE COMPLAINT

Central to the role of the FOS is the resolution of complaints. The concept of a 'complaint' is one that appears throughout DISP, so it makes sense to consider this first before going on to look at the FOS's jurisdiction (as to which, see the following chapters).

For most of DISP, 'complaints' are defined in the Glossary of the FCA Handbook as *'any oral or written expression of dissatisfaction'* about financial services, which:

- alleges that the complainant has suffered (or may suffer) financial loss, material distress or material inconvenience; and

- relates to an activity of that respondent, or of any other respondent with whom that respondent has some connection in marketing or providing financial services or products, which comes under the jurisdiction of the FOS.

This is intended to be a very broad definition,[1] and contains three elements: first, the communication of dissatisfaction to the firm; second, that the dissatisfaction be about the provision of financial services or a redress determination within the FOS's jurisdiction; and, third, a suggestion that the complainant has suffered or may suffer a loss.[2]

There needs to be some active expression of dissatisfaction by the customer. A customer's acceptance of an invitation to participate in a firm's review of interest rate hedging products (which the firm had agreed with the FCA to conduct) does not itself amount to a complaint.[3] Nor,

---

1 *R (British Bankers Association) v FSA* [2011] EWHC 99 (Admin) at [38].

2 *Davis v Lloyds Bank* [2021] EWCA Civ 557 at [44]. Notably, complaints about the conduct of a review process undertaken by a firm in agreement with the FCA does not fall within the FOS's jurisdiction: see Chapter 3.

3 *Davis v Lloyds Bank* [2021] EWCA Civ 557 at [25], citing *Day v Barclays Bank*

it seems, does a bare statement by a customer that they would have been better off if they had not entered into a relevant financial product.[4]

The FOS website explains that a complaint must first be made to '*the financial business you're unhappy with*' to give them a '*chance to sort things out before bringing your complaint to us… If you're not happy with the outcome of your complaint to the business, you can ask us to investigate what's happened.*'[5] Complaints can be pursued by phone,[6] online, or by the completion of a complaint form.

It is only after a customer has complained to the firm that they can complain to the FOS. As explained in Chapter 6, the firm has 8 weeks to respond to the complaint, by which time it ought to have provided the customer with information about complaining to the FOS.

If and when a complaint is made to the FOS, it will normally be made through the FOS's website, which will first ask the complainant to answer questions in an automated 'complaint checker', to check that the FOS has jurisdiction to consider the complaint. It then allows the complainant to enter details of their complaint in an online complaint form, or to call a telephone number.

Accordingly, the complaint can be in writing or by telephone. Even with written complaints, the FOS does not expect statements of case like those used in court proceedings. Complaints can be very informal, and the FOS is not limited to the complaint as formulated by the complainant. Instead, it may reach a decision on a basis other than that put forward by the complainant.[7] Indeed, it is part of the FOS's job to determine the

[2018] EWHC 393 (QB). The latter case held, at [28], that submissions within a review could not amount to a complaint, though also noted at [29] the claimant's position in that case that the review was not itself a complaint.

4 *Davis v Lloyds Bank* [2021] EWCA Civ 557 at [29] and [50].

5 http://www.financial-ombudsman.org.uk/consumer/complaints.htm.

6 As occurred in *R (Bankole) v FOS* [2012] EWHC 3555 (Admin). See [6].

7 *R (Green) v FOS* [2003] EWHC 338 (Admin) at [41].

nature of the complaint.[8]

The courts have considered it reasonable for the FOS to continue to assess a complaint, even when made in a 'somewhat tangled way'. In *R (Calland) v FOS* [2013] EWHC 1327 (Admin), the court accepted that the FOS was right to consider complaints, even though the 'expression of dissatisfaction' was made to the FCA (then FSA), which then took an active role in referring complaints to the FOS. The FOS contacted the individuals and the individuals asked that the complaint be dealt with. It was suggested by the firm that the FSA or the FOS had solicited the complaints.[9] The court had no doubt that the FOS was entitled to consider it.[10]

Likewise, *R (iDealing.com) v FOS* [2024] EWHC 847 (Admin) arose out of a complaint about one firm, where the FOS suggested that a complaint should be made against a further firm. The court confirmed that this was acceptable, in line with DISP 3.5.2G.[11]

It is not necessary for a complainant to pursue the complaint themselves if they authorise somebody else to do so.[12]

8 *R (Full Circle Asset Management Ltd) v FOS* [2017] EWHC 323 (Admin) at [53].

9 See [21] and [55].

10 At [57] and [120].

11 See [34]-[36].

12 DISP 2.7.2R.

CHAPTER THREE

THE FOS'S COMPULSORY AND VOLUNTARY JURISDICTIONS

The FOS can only hear complaints which are within its jurisdiction. The FOS comprises two jurisdictions:

1. The Compulsory Jurisdiction to which all firms authorised under FSMA (and certain unauthorised persons and former firms) carrying on activities specified by the FCA under the compulsory jurisdiction rules are compulsorily subject.

2. The Voluntary Jurisdiction to which persons (whether authorised or unauthorised) participate voluntarily in by contractual arrangement with FOS Ltd. Persons engaged in the voluntary jurisdiction are known as 'VJ Participants'.

According to DISP 2.2.1G, the scope of the FOS's two jurisdictions, and whether a complaint can therefore be dealt with by the FOS, depends on:

1. The type of activity to which the complaint relates, which this chapter considers further.[1]

2. The place where the activity to which the complaint relates was carried out (i.e. the FOS's territorial jurisdiction),[2] which we discuss in Chapter 4.

3. Whether the complainant is eligible,[3] for which see Chapter 5.

---

1 DISP 2.3, 2.4 and 2.5.

2 DISP 2.6.

3 DISP 2.7.

4. Whether the complaint was referred to the FOS in time,[4] for which see Chapter 6.

Despite the number of jurisdictional hurdles that a complainant must overcome, it should in most cases be clear when the FOS has jurisdiction and when it does not. As referred to in Chapter 2, the FOS's website has a 'complaint checker' that can be used to check whether a complaint can be pursued.

By DISP 3.2.1R, the FOS is required to determine whether a complaint is outside of its jurisdiction. In *R (Linear Investments Ltd) v FOS* [2024] EWHC 1428 (Admin), the court confirmed that this requires the FOS to consider issues whether or not they were raised by the complainant. In that case, jurisdiction depended on client classification, which the FOS concluded the firm had got wrong.

Whilst the FOS will take a view on whether it has jurisdiction, it will ultimately be for the courts to decide if the FOS got it right. It is a matter of statutory construction what the limits of the FOS's jurisdiction are, and if needs be they can be determined by way of judicial review (see Chapter 17).

The Compulsory Jurisdiction

As the name suggests, the Compulsory Jurisdiction sets out the mandatory jurisdiction of the FOS over some respondents and their activities.[5]

The FCA Handbook's Glossary provides a lengthy and broad definition of 'respondent'. As the FCA's jurisdiction has extended to cover various activities, so the definition has expanded. As a rule of thumb, it will often be sufficient to check that the relevant institution is listed on the FCA Register as a 'firm' (where that word is used expansively, beyond the formal definition as described below). 'Firm Status' explains the basis for

---

4 DISP 2.8.

5 FSMA, s.226.

the firm appearing in the Register.

There are some firms that are listed in the FCA's register but where the firm is not within the Compulsory Jurisdiction. One example is cryptoasset firms which, since 10 January 2020, have been required to register with the FCA under the Money Laundering Regulations. The FOS does not automatically have jurisdiction over such firms, unless they also fall within another, relevant, category.

The Compulsory Jurisdiction also covers respondents not contained on the FCA's register, including:

1. Complaints against businesses which were firms at the time of the events which were complained about.
2. Relevant complaints against former members of former schemes.[6]
3. Relevant credit-related complaints against businesses which were, at the time of the events complained about, covered by a standard licence under the Consumer Credit Act 1974.
4. Certain complaints against designated credit reference agencies under the Small and Medium Sized Business (Credit Information) Regulations 2015.[7]
5. Certain complaints against designated finance platforms under the Small and Medium Sized Business (Finance Platforms) Regulations 2015.[8]

FSMA, s. 226(4) provides that only 'regulated activities', or activities which could be made regulated activities, can be subject to the FOS's

6 Including under the Ombudsman Transitional Order, the Mortgage and General Insurance Complaints Transitional Order, the FSMA 2000 (Claims Management Activity) Order 2018, SI 2018/1253 (Claims Management Order) and the FSMA 2000 (Regulated Activities) (Amendment) Order 2021, SI 2021/90 (the Funeral Plans Order.

7 SI 2015/1945.

8 SI 2015/1946.

Compulsory Jurisdiction.[9]

Often there will be no dispute about the relevant activities. Most 'financial services' as usually described are covered, particularly those provided to retail customers. Accordingly, almost anything done by a bank, an insurance company or similar institution will be capable of being considered by the FOS. Matters become more complicated away from that central scenario and have led to the FOS and the courts grappling with questions such as whether tax advice also constitutes financial advice.[10]

DISP 2.1.4R defines carrying on activity as including: (i) '*offering, providing or failing to provide a service in relation to an activity*'; (ii) '*administering or failing to administer a service in relation to an activity*'; and (iii) '*the manner in which a respondent has administered its business, provided that the business is an activity subject to the [FOS] jurisdiction*'.

This is cast in very broad language but is not unlimited. The service or conduct subject to a complaint must be '*in relation to*' an activity or related to the '*manner in which*' the respondent carries out business. Complaints about wholly ancillary activities that have nothing to do with how the respondent carries on its business will not be caught by the FOS's jurisdiction. The definition of activity also puts beyond doubt that a failure to do something is caught just as much as a positive act is.

The remainder of this chapter outlines the different activities that are within the scope of, and can be considered by the FOS under, the Compulsory Jurisdiction.

---

9 Regulated activities are defined by FSMA, s.22 and set out in the Financial Services and Markets Act 2000 (Regulated Activities) Order 2001, more commonly referred to as 'the RAO'.

10 *R (Chancery (UK) LLP) v FOS* [2015] EWHC 407 (Admin).

Firms

In this book, we sometimes use the word 'firm' in an informal sense to refer to the business in respect of which there is a complaint.

However, for the purpose of jurisdiction, there is a more formal definition. A firm is an 'authorised person' – namely a firm that has been authorised by the FCA under Part 4A of FSMA. The FCA register lists these firms as 'authorised'. This category includes the vast majority of banks, insurance companies and other traditional financial institutions, and also members of Lloyds of London.

The fact that a firm falls within the Compulsory Jurisdiction is not sufficient to ensure that the FOS has jurisdiction over a complaint. The FCA Register emphasises this in text on each firm's entry, with a warning that some activities by the firm 'may not be protected', meaning that customers cannot rely on the FOS or the Financial Services Compensation Scheme (the 'FSCS'). The warning suggests that: '*If you would like to check what is and what isn't covered, you can ask this firm to confirm this to you in writing.*' However, the firm's own view is not definitive: ultimately it is a question of law whether a particular activity falls within the FOS's jurisdiction.

A list of activities covered by the Compulsory Jurisdiction is set out in DISP 2.3.1R, and covers 'firms' (properly so-called, i.e., those authorised under Part 4A of FSMA) carrying on one or more of the following:

1. **Regulated activities other than auction regulation bidding.** A consideration of what constitutes a 'regulated activity' is outside the scope of this book. For the most part, the reader will be able to find a list in the Glossary of the FCA Handbook.[11] The more important will include: (i) accepting deposits; (ii) effecting / carrying out contracts of insurance; (iii) dealing in investments as agent or principal, or arranging deals in investments; (iv) advising on investments; and (v) arranging regulated mortgage contracts.

[11] Full consideration of 'regulated activities' will also need to focus on the provisions of the RAO.

2. **Payment services.** This covers those activities caught by the Payment Services Regulations.[12] Many day-to-day retail banking activities associated with operating current accounts will be caught, as will money remittance services.[13]

3. **Consumer buy-to-let ('CBTL') business.** In other words, acting as a buy to let lender, arranger or adviser, as each of those terms are defined in the Glossary to the FCA Handbook.

4. **Lending money secured by a charge on land.**

5. **Lending money.** However this does not cover providing 'restricted credit' insofar as this is not a 'credit-related regulated activity'.[14] By way of explanation, 'restricted credit' refers to loans from a firm to a consumer which can only be used to pay a supplier as a result of an existing arrangement between a supplier and a firm. A common example might include financing arrangements between car dealers and finance companies. The definition of 'restricted credit' does not include loans secured by charges over land or payments by plastic cards (as long as they are not store cards).

6. **Paying money by a plastic card which is not a store card where this is not a credit-related regulated activity.**

7. **Providing ancillary banking services**, including things such as operating cash machines, foreign currency exchanges, safe deposit boxes and account aggregation services.[15]

8. **Offering and/or issuing of investments by insurance special**

---

[12] The relevant regulations depend on the date of the activity in question: if it occurred on before 13 January 2018 the Payment Services Regulations 2009 are applicable. After that date, see the Payment Services Regulations 2017.

[13] A list is provided in reg. 2(1) and Schedule 1 of the relevant regulations.

[14] A list of 'credit-related regulated activities' can be found in Parts II and IIIA of the RAO (especially arts. 26A, 36H, 39D, 39E, 39F, 39G, 53DA, 60B, 60N, 89A and 89B).

[15] DISP 2.1.5G.

purpose vehicles.

6. **Giving non-personal recommendation advice.** This covers the regulated activity specified in art.53(1) of the Financial Services and Markets Act 2000 (Regulated Activities) Order 2001 (the 'RAO') and which does not amount to a personal recommendation.

Activities that are 'ancillary' to these activities are also caught. DISP 2.3.1R states that advice in connection with any of the activities above is ancillary to it.

Investment firms, CRD credit institutions and CPMI firms

Under DISP 2.3.1AR, the FOS also has jurisdiction to consider a complaint under the Compulsory Jurisdiction if it relates to an act or omission by:

1. An investment firm authorised under the UK provisions that implemented the MiFID II Directive when providing investments services or ancillary services.

2. A 'CRD credit institution' when providing one or more investment services. These are particular types of credit institutions with a registered office or head office in the UK.

3. An investment firm authorised under the UK provisions that implemented the MiFID II Directive or a CRD credit institution when selling structured deposits to clients or advising clients on them.

4. A collective portfolio management firm ('CPMI') when providing the activities permitted by the UK provisions that implemented Article 6(3) of the UCITS Directive.

5. A CPMI firm when providing the activities permitted by the UK provisions that implemented Article 6(4) of the Alternative Investment Fund Managers Directive ('AIFMD').

For the purposes of this rule, the FOS can consider a complaint about an act carried out by a MiFID investment firm that is preparatory to the provision of an investment service or ancillary service which is an integral part of such a service. For example, this includes generic advice given by a MiFID investment firm to a client prior to, or in the course of, the provision of investment advice or another investment service or ancillary service.[16]

Payment service providers and electronic money issuers

These are covered by DISP 2.3.2AR and 2.3.2BR.

In broad terms, a payment service provider ('PSP') is a company that allows the making of electronic payments. They act as intermediaries between those how make payments and those who accept them. Examples of PSPs include Apple Card or Apple Pay, PayPal and WorldPay.[17] The FOS can consider a complaint under the Compulsory Jurisdiction if it relates to an act or omission by a PSP in carrying on any of the following:

1. Payment services;

2. Regulated consumer credit activities;

3. Any ancillary activities, including advice, carried on by the PSP in connection with payments services or regulated consumer

16 DISP 2.3.1BG.

17 A payment service provider is defined in the Glossary to the FCA Handbook as including for the purposes of DISP: (a) an authorised payment institution; (b) a small payment institution; (c) a registered account information service provider; (d) an EEA registered account information service provider, (e) an electronic money issuer; (f) the Post Office Limited; (g) the Bank of England, other than when acting in its capacity as a monetary authority or carrying out other functions of a public nature; and (h) government departments and local authorities, other than when carrying out functions of a public nature.

credit activities.[18]

In addition, DISP 2.3.5G explains that the Compulsory Jurisdiction in respect of PSPs includes complaints about: (i) the UK end of a 'one leg' payment services transaction – namely, services provided from UK establishments that also involve a PSP located outside the EEA; and (ii) payment services, irrespective of the currency of the transaction.

Electronic money issuers ('EMIs') are entities authorised to issue electronic money and provide payment services such as domestic and international electronic funds transfers and provide bank accounts and e-wallets.[19] Similar to PSPs, the FOS can consider a complaint under the Compulsory Jurisdiction if it relates to an act or omission by an EMI in carrying on any of the following:

1. Issuing e-money.
2. Regulated consumed credit activities.
3. Any ancillary activities, including advice, carried on by the EMI in connection with the issuance of e-money or regulated consumer credit activities.[20]

Consumer buy-to-let firms

DISP 2.3.2BAR provides that the FOS has jurisdiction over complaints relating to acts and omissions by CBTL firms carrying on CBTL (i.e. consumer buy-to-let) business.

---

18 DISP 2.3.2AR.

19 The definition of electronic money issuer in the Glossary to the FCA Handbook follows a similar format to the definition of PSPs, including amongst others authorised and small electronic money institutions, as well as their EEA authorised counterparts.

20 DISP 2.3.2BR.

Designated credit reference agencies and designated finance platforms

By DISP 2.3.2DR, the FOS can consider complaints under the compulsory jurisdiction if related to acts or omissions by designated credit reference agencies and finance platforms in carrying on either (i) the activity of providing credit information;[21] or (ii) ancillary activities thereto (including advice).

A 'designated credit reference agency' is one which is designated under Reg. 9 of the Small and Medium Sized Business Regulations 2015. These Regulations impose various obligations and duties on credit reference agencies to provide credit information about small and medium sized businesses. The three main consumer credit reference agencies in the UK are Equifax, Experian and TransUnion.[22]

Consumer Credit Jurisdiction

Prior to 1 April 2014, the FOS had a consumer credit jurisdiction. This was given to the FOS by s.226A of FSMA. It covered complaints in connection with consumer credit activities by respondents who were authorised under s.34A of the Consumer Credit Act 1974.

The consumer credit jurisdiction was (prior to 1 April 2014) set out in DISP 2.4.1R. The FOS had jurisdiction under its consumer credit jurisdiction if: (i) it was not covered by the compulsory jurisdiction; and (ii) it related to an act or omission by a licensee in carrying on either consumer credit activities or ancillary activities thereto.

'Consumer credit activities' were defined in the Glossary as meaning, amongst other things: (i) providing credit / being a creditor under a regulated consumer credit agreement; (ii) the bailment of goods under a regulated consumer hire agreement; and (iii) certain credit brokerage activities.

---

21 Small and Medium Sized Business (Credit Information) Regulations 2015.

22 According to the Information Commissioners' Office: https://ico.org.uk/for-the-public/credit/.

However, that jurisdiction no longer has a separate existence. To prevent complainants from finding themselves without a right of recourse, transitional provisions were implemented.[23]

A complaint made on or after 1 April 2014 which relates to an act or omission before that date will be dealt with under the s.226 jurisdiction if: (i) it could have been dealt with under s.226A (disregarding whether the complainant would have been eligible under the rules made for the purposes of the consumer credit jurisdiction and whether the complaint would have fallen within a description specified in those rules); (ii) the complainant is eligible; and (iii) the complainant wishes to have their complaint dealt with under the scheme.[24]

Firms and unauthorised persons subject to a former scheme

The FOS has jurisdiction over certain complaints that previously belonged (pre-2001) to the FOS's predecessors and also the General Insurance Council and Mortgage Code Arbitration Scheme (prior to 2005 and 2004 respectively). Transitional arrangements exist for these former schemes, but they are now of largely historical interest. If relevant, see DISP 2.3.2G.

Mixed activities

Some services provided may cover a number of elements. A particular issue has arisen where the consumer is advised to invest in unregulated products, but in a manner that also concerns regulated products.

In *R (Tenetconnect Services) v FOS* [2018] EWHC 459 (Admin), a consumer was advised to sell regulated investments (an insurance policy, and bonds) in order to invest in property in Goa. The firm argued that the 'regulated' piece of advice caused no loss, and it could not be held liable for the 'unregulated' advice. This argument was dismissed: where

23 DISP 2.3.2-AG and the Financial Services and Markets Act 2000 (Regulated Activities) (Amendment) (No.2) Order 2013, Art 11.

24 DISP 2.3.2AG.

the buying and selling of property is intrinsically linked, the advice is regulated and the FOS has jurisdiction.

Albeit in a different context, the courts have taken the same view where regulated mortgages have funded unregulated investments,[25] and transfers into a self-invested pension plan, to purchase unregulated products within that plan.[26]

Consumer redress schemes

One of the FCA's more important regulatory tools can be found in FSMA, s. 404. This gives it the power to set up consumer redress schemes if amongst other things it appears to the FCA that '*there may have been a widespread or regular failure by relevant firms to comply with requirements applicable to the carrying on by them of any activity*'.

Obviously, it is necessary to ensure that the consumers who have a right to redress pursuant to a s. 404 scheme are adequately protected when determinations under them are made. To that end, FSMA s. 404B(11) and DISP 2.3.2C G provide that a complainant who (i) is not satisfied with a redress determination made by a respondent under a consumer redress scheme; or (ii) considers that a respondent has failed to make a redress determination in accordance with a consumer redress scheme can be heard by the FOS.

The FOS has jurisdiction to consider such complaints as follows:

1. A complaint can only be referred under DISP 2.3.2CG if made by a 'complainant'.

2. The term 'consumer redress scheme' is defined for the purposes of the Handbook as one imposed under FSMA s. 404 on authorised persons, payment service providers or electronic money issuers. It also includes those imposed on a particular firm, payment service provider or electronic money issuer by a

[25] *Emptage v FSCS* [2013] EWCA Civ 729.

[26] *Adams v Options UK Personal Pensions* [2021] EWCA Civ 474 4.

requirement of its authorisation. This is a slightly different definition from that used in s.404.

3. The FOS's jurisdiction under these provisions relates to 'redress determinations'. This is tightly defined as a written communication from a respondent under a consumer redress scheme which: (i) sets out the results of the respondent's determination under the scheme; (ii) encloses a copy of the FOS's standard explanatory leaflet; and (iii) informs the complainant that if he is dissatisfied, he may make a complaint to the FOS and must do so within 6 months.

If a complaint is to be made about a redress scheme, the requirements of DISP 2.3.2CG must be fulfilled. This can be seen from *R (Mazarona Properties Ltd) v FOS* [2017] EWHC 1135 (Admin), which related to a bank's review of interest rate hedging products under an agreement with the FCA. As this was not a consumer redress scheme under FSMA, s. 404, the FOS did not have jurisdiction under the provisions discussed above.

Section 404B of FSMA also makes provision for how awards should be made under this head of jurisdiction. In particular, s. 404B(4) grants the FOS the power to decide what the determination under the redress scheme ought to have been. This can include ordering a money payment, in which case the order must not exceed the FOS's usual monetary limit (see Chapter 13). The FOS also has the power to order that respondents take specific actions (s.404B (8)).

Appointed Representatives

Complaints about acts or omissions include those in respect of activities for which the relevant person is responsible, including the business of any appointed representative or agent, for which that person has accepted responsibility.[27]

There may be a question of whether the principal has accepted

27 DISP 2.3.3G.

responsibility for the activity complained about. Under s.39 of FSMA, appointed representatives are exempt from responsibility for such activities provided that they are: (a) party to a contract with an authorised person ('his principal') which: (i) permits or requires him to carry on business of a prescribed description, and (ii) complies with such requirements as may be prescribed; and (b) is someone for whose activities in carrying on the whole or part of that business his principal has accepted responsibility in writing.

In *Anderson v Sense Network* [2019] EWCA Civ 1395, the court held that principals were permitted, under section 39, to authorise the whole *or part* of a regulated activity. Principals would only be liable for business which they had permitted under their written agreement. A principal would not therefore be liable for activities undertaken by an appointed representative outside of the agreement.[28]

In this context, the courts distinguish between contractual limitations on 'what' the appointed representative may do (which does limit the principal's liability) and limitations on 'how' the appointed representative may provide the services that are permitted (which will not limit the principal's liability). If a contract states that an appointed representative may not deal with retail clients, for example, this is considered to be a 'how' question and will not prevent the principal from being liable for advice to retail clients.[29]

The Voluntary Jurisdiction

Even if the FOS does not have jurisdiction under the compulsory scheme, it may have jurisdiction under the voluntary scheme.

The statutory basis for this can be found in s.227 of FSMA, which sets out the requirements for a complaint to be heard under the scheme. They are that:

---

28 See [37]–[57].

29 *KVB Consultants v Jacob Hopkins McKenzie* [2024] EWCA Civ 765 (Comm).

1. The complainant is eligible and wishes to have the complaint dealt with under the scheme.

2. At the time the act or omission is said to have occurred, the respondent was participating in the scheme.

3. At the time the complaint is referred under the scheme, the respondent has not withdrawn from the scheme in accordance with its provisions.

4. The act or omission to which the complaint relates occurred when the voluntary jurisdiction rules were in force in relation to the activity in question.

5. The complaint cannot be dealt with under the compulsory jurisdiction.

These requirements are elaborated on in DISP 2.5.1R. In order for a complaint to be brought under the voluntary jurisdiction, it must be in respect of what DISP calls a 'VJ participant'. These are entities which have signed up to the FOS's jurisdiction by contractual agreement. They include certain banks, insurance companies, investment companies, mortgage and insurance intermediaries, amongst others. Unfortunately, the FOS website does not maintain a list of VJ participants, but the FOS's 2024/25 Plans and Budget indicated that it receives 13,000 complaints under the voluntary jurisdiction each year (out of a total of 192,500).

DISP 2.5.1R sets out certain restrictions on the types of activity to which the voluntary jurisdiction applies. It must not be covered by the compulsory jurisdiction and it must be one of the following:

1. An activity carried on after 28 April 1988 that was not regulated at the time of the act or omission complained of, but was so regulated when the VJ participant joined the scheme (or became an authorised person, whichever is the later). As explained in DISP 2.5.3G, the purpose of this provision is to ensure that activities that would be covered by the compulsory jurisdiction but which are not covered by the transitional provisions in DISP 2.3.2R are caught.

2. A financial services activity (which term is undefined) carried on after commencement of s.19 FSMA (1 December 2001) by a VJ participant which was covered in respect of that activity by a former scheme immediately before the commencement of s.19 FSMA.

3. Most activities which as at 1 August 2022 would be covered by the compulsory jurisdiction if carried out from a UK establishment. A list of these activities (of which there are many) can be found in DISP 2, Annex 1G.

4. An activity which would be a regulated claims management activity and would be covered by the Compulsory Jurisdiction if it were carried on in Great Britain.

5. Lending money secured by a charge on land.

6. Lending money other than restricted credit where that is not a credit-related regulated activity.

7. Paying money by a plastic card (excluding a store card where that is not a credit-related regulated activity).

8. Providing ancillary banking services.

9. Acting as an intermediary for a loan secured by a charge over land.

10. Acting as an intermediary for general insurance business or long-term insurance business.

11. National Savings and Investments' business.

12. Offering and/or issuing of investments by insurance special purpose vehicles.

Or in any case ancillary activities (including advice) carried on by the VJ participant in connection with the above.

DISP 2.5.5R provides that the voluntary jurisdiction covers acts or omissions that occurred before the VJ participant was participating in the voluntary jurisdiction and also irrespective of whether the act or omission occurred before or after 1 December 2001,[30] if either the complaint could have been dealt with under a former scheme or it has been agreed in the standard terms pursuant to which the VJ participants partake in the voluntary jurisdiction.[31]

As can be seen, the scope of the voluntary jurisdiction is broad. There may be some overlap with the compulsory jurisdiction,[32] in which case that jurisdiction takes precedence.

30 Referred to in the rules simply as 'commencement'.

31 The terms are made under FSMA, Schedule 17, paragraph 18.

32 DISP 2.5.2G.

CHAPTER FOUR

THE FOS'S TERRITORIAL JURISDICTION

In this chapter, we consider the FOS's territorial jurisdiction. The essence of the FOS's jurisdiction is that it will only apply if the activities in question were carried out by a UK establishment.

It is necessary, however, to distinguish between the compulsory and voluntary jurisdictions.

Compulsory jurisdiction

The relevant provisions here are DISP 2.6.1R and 2.6.2AG.

The FOS will not have jurisdiction unless the activities in question are carried out from a UK establishment (except for regulated claims managed activities and ancillary activities, which must be carried on in Great Britain).

It is enough for the appointed representatives under s.39 of FSMA to carry on business from such a UK establishment, in which case the principal firm is within the FOS's jurisdiction.

In the case of payment service providers or electronic money issuers, it is enough that their agencies carry on business from such an establishment.

For the FOS to have jurisdiction the business in question must be carried on from the relevant establishment. It is not enough that a respondent has a UK establishment if the complaint relates to business that was carried on from an establishment outside the UK.

Voluntary Jurisdiction

The position under the voluntary jurisdiction is even more restrictive. The VJ participant must either carry on the activities in question from an establishment in the UK, alternatively in the EEA or Gibraltar where the following conditions are met: (i) the activity must be directed wholly or partly at the UK; (ii) any contracts concerning the activity must be governed by the law of England and Wales, Scotland or Northern Ireland;[1] and (iii) the VJ participant must have notified 'appropriate regulators' in the place of its establishment that it intends to participate in the voluntary jurisdiction.[2]

This last requirement has the potential to cause unfairness when the participant has not given the appropriate notice and is therefore able to avoid the FOS's jurisdiction.

Does it make a difference if the complainant is outside the UK?

The answer here is a clear 'no': see DISP 2.6.5G. There is no requirement that a complainant lives or is based in the UK.

1 The rules for determining the choice of law of a contract will be governed by the Rome I Regulation 593/2008 (as retained in UK law following Brexit).

2 DISP 2.6.4R.

CHAPTER FIVE

WHO IS AN ELIGIBLE COMPLAINANT?

A complaint may only be considered by the FOS if it is brought by or on behalf of an eligible complainant.[1] There are two requirements for the complainant to be eligible:

The first is the 'who' requirement: is the complainant someone that can bring a complaint before the FOS?

The second is the 'relationship' requirement: is the complainant complaining about a relevant relationship?

The 'who' requirement: the complainant

DISP 2.7.3R provides a list of eligible complainants. It must be a person[2] that is either: (i) a consumer; (ii) a micro-enterprise; (iii) a small charity; (iv) a trustee of a small trust; (v) a CBTL customer; (vi) a small business; and (vii) a guarantor.

We discuss each type of eligible complainant below.

---

1 DISP 2.7.1R. To bring a complaint on behalf of an eligible complainant, the person bringing the complaint must be authorised to do so either by the eligible complainant or by law. The person authorised to complain on the complainant's behalf does not themselves need to be an eligible complainant: DISP 2.7.2R.

2 Which includes for these purposes any natural or legal person, including a body corporate or unincorporated, and partnerships.

A consumer

This means an individual acting for the purposes which are wholly or mainly outside that individual's trade, business, craft or profession.[3]

In *R (Bluefin Insurance Services Ltd) v FOS* [2014] EWHC 3413 (Admin), Wilkie J considered this definition in the context of a director of a company who benefited from a Directors and Officers policy and who sought to complain to the FOS. It was held that he was not a consumer as his company had advanced his business interests and the policy covered his acts as a director. Thus, '*the subject matter of his complaint was wholly concerned with the potential loss arising from lack of insurance cover in respect of a liability which he had incurred in the course of his trade, business, or profession.*'[4]

This conclusion rested on a different definition of consumer from that which now applies[5], but there is no reason to think that the current definition would have led to a different result.

DISP refers not only to those acts wholly outside a person's trade but also covers those which are '*mainly*' outside their business. This adds a degree of uncertainty into what is meant by a 'consumer', as some connection with business interests may be permissible.

The business connection, if any, should be ancillary and minimal. The presence of a business connection and whether an individual could be defined as a 'consumer' was considered in *Ashfaq v International Insurance Co. of Hannover PLC* [2017] EWCA Civ 357, in the different context of the Unfair Terms in Consumer Contracts Regulations 1999 and ICOBS

3 The Glossary provides that 'consumer' has different meanings in different parts of the FCA Handbook. Paragraph 7 of that definition applies for the purposes of DISP 2.7.3R. The definition is adopted from Regulation 3 of the Alternative Dispute Resolution for Consumer Disputes (Competent Authorities and Information) Regulations 2015 (SI 2015/542).

4 See [125].

5 'Consumer' at the material time and considered in *R (Bluefin)* was defined as '*any natural person acting for purposes outside his trade, business or profession*': see *R (Bluefin)* at [20].

2.1.1G(2) and 8.1.2R. In ICOBS 2.1.1G(2) and 8.1.2R 'consumer' was defined as someone acting mainly for purposes unrelated to their trade or profession. It was held that there was no real prospect of a claimant who was using a property covered by insurance for the business of letting to students establishing that he was a consumer.

It is also of note that the definition of consumer refers to an 'individual'. This should exclude, for instance, companies and partnerships[6] from the definition.

Micro-enterprises[7]

A micro-enterprise is an enterprise that employs fewer than 10 persons and has a turnover or annual balance sheet that does not exceed 2 million.[8]

An enterprise is defined as including any person engaged in economic activity whatever the legal form. This is evidently intended to be a broad definition. It will catch self-employed individuals, family businesses engaged in craft or other activities, and partnerships or associations regularly engaged in economic activities.[9]

The time at which it is assessed whether the requirements of being a micro-enterprise are fulfilled will depend on what the complaint is about.

---

6 For the difficulties relating to how regulatory rules can apply to partnerships, see *Thomas v Triodos* [2017] EWHC 314 (QB) at [58].

7 There is a dedicated website for complaints made by or on behalf of micro-enterprises and small businesses, which includes links to data on complaints made by micro-enterprises: https://sme.financial-ombudsman.org.uk/.

8 The definition of 'micro-enterprise' in the Glossary to the FCA Handbook notes that, in determining whether these criteria are met, Articles 3 to 6 of the Annex to 'Commission Recommendation 2003/361/EC concerning the definition of micro, small and medium-sized enterprises' must be applied.

9 By way of example, this would presumably cover an unincorporated association comprised of volunteers running (say) a museum, provided that at least some form of economic activity was carried on (perhaps the invariable café or gift shop, no matter how small).

By DISP 2.7.3R(2), if the complaint relates wholly or partly to payments services, it must be at the time of the conclusion of the payment service contract or at the time the complainant refers the complaint to the respondent. Otherwise, it must be at the time the complaint is referred to the respondent.

DISP 2.7.4G states that when assessing whether an enterprise is a micro-enterprise, account should be taken of the enterprise's partners or linked enterprises.[10] So if a parent company of the complainant does not meet the definition of a micro-enterprise, the complainant will not do so either.

Small charities

A charity is an eligible complainant if it has an annual income of less than £6.5 million at the time the complaint is referred to the respondent.[11] No further definitions or guidance are provided.

Trustees of small trusts

A trustee of a trust will be an eligible complainant if the trust that has a net asset value of less than £5 million at the time the complainant refers the complaint to the respondent.[12]

Consumer Buy-to-Let ('CBTL') consumers

In relation to a CBTL agreement, eligible complainants are 'CBTL consumers', defined in the Glossary as either: (i) persons acting for purposes that are outside their trade, business or profession, or; (ii) a borrower under a CBTL credit agreement.

---

[10] As those terms are defined in Recommendation 2003/361/EC of the Commission of 6th May 2003.

[11] DISP 2.7.3R.

[12] DISP 2.7.3R(4).

Note that, here, we are concerned with a 'person' (which will include companies and other legal entities) rather than just 'individuals. It is also noteworthy that, unlike with the definition of 'consumer', the fact that the person is acting for purposes that are in any way connected with their business will be fatal to the suggestion they are a CBTL consumer under the first limb of the test.

Small Businesses

Since April 2019, small businesses are also deemed eligible complainants. A complainant is considered eligible as a small business if, at the time of the complaint, they are not a micro-enterprise (as defined above); have an annual turnover of less than £6.5 million (or its equivalent in any other currency) and (a) employs fewer than 50 persons or (b) has a balance sheet total of less than £5 million (or its equivalent in any other currency).

As with micro-enterprises, the annex to 'Commission Recommendation 2003/361/EC concerning the definition of micro, small and medium-sized enterprises' must be applied when determining whether these criteria are met.

In March 2023, the FCA published a 'Call for Input survey' to consider whether the criteria for small businesses should be broadened to expand the scope of small businesses, which would be deemed eligible complainants. In publishing the Call for Input, the FCA noted that COVID-19 and the rising cost of living have affected how some small businesses operate.

In October 2023, the FCA published a feedback statement[13] on the findings from its review and concluded that the current threshold criteria for small businesses struck the appropriate balance between providing access to the FOS to small businesses that do not have the resources to resolve financial services disputes through the legal system and broadening this access to far. Accordingly, the FCA stated it would not

13 FCA Feedback Statement 'Findings of review of rules extending SME access to the Financial Ombudsman Service' (October 2023): https://www.fca.org.uk/publication/feedback/fs23-5.pdf.

be making changes to the definition for the purposes of DISP.

Guarantors

A complainant is eligible if they are a guarantor. For these purposes, 'guarantor' is an individual who is not a consumer[14] and has given a guarantee or security in respect of an obligation or liability of a person which was a micro-enterprise or small business, as at the date that the guarantee or security was given.

A guarantor shall be an eligible complainant only to the extent that their complaint arises from matters relevant to the relationship with the respondent referred to in DISP 2.7.6R(10)[15], which includes that the complainant gave the respondent a guarantee or security for a mortgage, a loan, an actual or prospective credit agreement, an actual or prospective regulated consumer hire agreement or any linked transaction as defined in the Consumer Credit Act 1974.

Applying the definitions

Factually, working out whether a complainant is within the various requirements above may be quite difficult.

Whilst many companies could be expected to keep good accounting records (making it easier to tell if they are a 'micro-enterprise' for instance), that will not always be so. Doubtless aware of these potential difficulties, DISP 2.7.5G warns respondent firms that if in doubt they should treat a complainant as if they were eligible. The FOS will then later determine eligibility by reference to appropriate evidence, such as audited accounts or VAT returns.

If a respondent firm is going to take a point on eligibility, they would do well to do so as soon as possible and make that clear (for instance, explaining to the would-be complainant that they will deal with them on

[14] As defined for the purposes of DISP.

[15] DISP 2.7.5AR.

a basis that is without prejudice to their right to dispute eligibility).

It has been said the question of whether a complainant is eligible is one of 'objective fact' and 'hard-edged criteria'.[16] This means that, on a judicial review arising out of a determination whether a complainant is eligible, the court will be able to decide the question for itself.

The relationship requirement

Even if a complainant is eligible, they must still fulfil the relationship requirement set out in DISP 2.7.6R. Essentially, the complaint must arise '*from matters relevant to one or more of the following relationships with the respondent*'.

There are 24 categories of relationships listed. The most important are likely to be as follows:

1. A customer, payment service user or electronic money holder of the respondent.[17] Also covered are potential customers, payment service users or electronic money holders.[18] Of these three terms, 'customer' is in practice the most important. It is defined in the Glossary to the FCA Handbook in a number of different ways depending on the activity in question, though in most cases the answer will be clear.

2. A payer in a payment transaction in relation to which the respondent is or was the payee's payment service provider, provided the complaint relates to the respondent's obligations under regulation 90(3) of the Payment Service Regulations 2017.[19] Regulation 90(3) concerns circumstances where the unique identifier provided by a payment service user is incorrect. A payee's payment service provider is required to cooperate with

16 See *R (Bluefin Insurance Services Ltd) v FOS* [2014] EWHC 3414 (Admin).

17 DISP 2.7.6R (1), (16) and (17).

18 DISP 2.7.6R (2).

19 DISP 2.7.8R(2A).

the payer's payment service provider to recover funds.

3. A person who has transferred funds as a result of an alleged authorised push payment fraud[20] and both: (i) the respondent is or was involved in the transfer of the funds; and (ii) the complaint is not a PSD complaint.[21]

4. A person for whose benefit a contract of insurance was or was intended to be taken out with or through the respondent.[22] This is not limited to just the person who was a party to the insurance contract. Many home, motor or travel insurance policies will be taken out for the benefit of family members by one member of the household. The expansive definition of eligible complainant avoids knotty issues about who strictly was a party to the contract. DISP 2.7.7G gives the further example of employees who have the benefit of a group permanent health policy taken out by an employer for their benefit.

5. Persons who have a right to benefit from a claim under a contract of insurance.[23] The rule refers to claims being 'devolved' by contract, assignment, subrogation or legislation, and allows those with claims under the Third Parties (Rights against Insurers) Act

---

20 Authorised push payment fraud is defined in the Glossary of the FCA Handbook as '*a transfer of funds by person A to person B, other than a transfer initiated by or through person B, where: (1) A intended to transfer the funds to a person other than B but was instead deceived into transferring the funds to B; or (2) A transferred funds to B for what they believed were legitimate purposes but which were in fact fraudulent.*'

21 DISP 2.7.6R(2B). A PSD complaint is defined in the Glossary of the FCA Handbook as '*any oral or written expression of dissatisfaction, whether justified or not, from, or on behalf of, a payment service user about the provision of, or failure to provide, a financial service or a redress determination: (a) which alleges the complainant has suffered (or may suffer) financial loss, material distress or material inconvenience; and (b) concerning the rights and obligations arising under Parts 6 and 7 of the Payment Services Regulations.*'

22 DISP 2.6.7R (5).

23 DISP 2.7.6R (6).

2010 to complain to the FOS.[24]

6. A person who gave the respondent a guarantee or security for a mortgage, loan, an actual or prospective regulated credit agreement, or any linked transaction under the Consumer Credit Act 1974.[25]

7. A person about whom information relevant to his financial standing is or was held by the respondent in providing credit references or credit information.[26] 'Providing credit references' concerns the furnishing of persons with information relevant to the financial standing of individuals or relevant recipients of credit, provided the information has been collected for that purpose.[27] 'Credit information' is defined to cover various items of information about sterling loans, sterling credit card accounts, sterling current accounts, as well as certain ancillary information.[28] DISP 2.7.6R(11B) also adds to the list of eligible complainants a person about whom 'specified information'[29] in relation to a 'finance application' was provided.[30]

8. A person from whom the respondent has sought to recover payment under a credit agreement or consumer hire agreement, irrespective of whether the respondent is a party to the

24 See, for example, Decision Reference DRN-2429231.

25 DISP 2.7.6R (10).

26 DISP 2.7.6R (11) and (11A).

27 This phrase has the same meaning as the activity specified in art.89B of the RAO.

28 Small and Medium Sized Business (Credit Information) Regulations 2015, in particular reg. 2 and Schedule 1.

29 As that term is defined in reg.2 and Schedule 1 of the Small and Medium Sized Business (Finance Platforms) Regulations 2015/1946. Essentially, it covers the name of the business, its address, email address, phone number, the amount of finance requested, the type of finance, its legal structure, the duration of its trading, and the date by which it requires or has requested finance.

30 As that term is also defined in reg. 2 of the Small and Medium Sized Business (Finance Platforms) Regulations 2015/1946. Essentially, a request in any form for a finance facility.

agreement.[31] A complainant is also covered where the respondent has sought to exercise or enforce rights on behalf of a creditor or owner under a credit agreement or consumer hire agreement in carrying on debt administration.[32]

A person authorised by law

Even if the complainant does not strictly satisfy the eligibility requirements, they may be able to rely on DISP 2.7.2R. This is a narrow rule, which provides that a complaint may be brought on behalf of an eligible complainant or a deceased person that would have been eligible. The person bringing the complaint must, however, be authorised by someone who would be an eligible complainant or be authorised 'by law'. The term 'by law' has presumably been added to cover, for instance, the executor of an estate. In these circumstances, the person so authorised need not themselves be an eligible complainant.

Where the complainant authorises another to act, the position is straightforward. Provided that there is evidence of the authorisation, the rules allow anybody to act. Typical examples include lawyers acting for complainants, or family members.

Authority 'by law' is not defined, but in *Shop Direct Finance Co v Official Receiver* [2023] EWCA Civ 367 it was common ground that it extends to trustees in bankruptcy. It was explained in that case that the phrase '*on behalf of*' refers to persons able to complain '*in place of*' the original complainant.[33] This concept would presumably extend to those entitled to act through a power of attorney, or a court-appointed deputy under the Mental Capacity Act 2005. The rule also allows for complaints pursued by the personal representatives of deceased customers.

There is also a narrow exception to the eligibility rules under the FOS's transitional provisions: where a complainant who wishes to bring a

31 DISP 2.7.6R (12)(a).

32 Debt administration is a regulated activity defined by Art.39G of the RAO.

33 See [21].

complaint is not otherwise eligible, but could have brought a complaint under one of the former schemes that the FOS assumed responsibility for, they may be treated by the FOS as if they were eligible.[34] This is now of largely historical interest.

Exceptions

Even if a complainant would otherwise be eligible, they may fall within one of the eligibility exceptions contained in DISP 2.7.9R to 2.7.10G.

First, entities that are themselves firms, payment service providers, electronic money issuers, CBTL firms, designated credit reference agencies, designated finance platforms, or VJ participants who wish to bring a complaint in respect of activities which they are authorised to carry on are excluded.[35]

Secondly, in connection with the compulsory jurisdiction, a complainant will be ineligible if they are either a professional client or eligible counterparty in relation to the firm and activity in question at the time of the act or omission subject to the complaint.[36]

The terms 'professional client' or 'eligible counterparty' are references to the classification rules contained in COBS 3.5 and 3.6. A client will normally either be a retail client, professional client or eligible counterparty. The purpose of these rules is to change the degree of regulation by reference to how sophisticated the customer is.

A professional client will be a client that is either a *per se* professional client or an elective professional client.

Per se professional clients include authorised firms, insurance companies

[34] DISP 2.7.8G, arising out of the Financial Services and Markets Act 2000 (Transitional Provisions) (Ombudsman Scheme and Complaints Scheme) Order 2001 or the Financial Services and Markets Act 2000 (Transitional Provisions) (Complaints Relating to General Insurance and Mortgages) Order 2004.

[35] DISP 2.7.9R (1).

[36] Except if they are a trustee of a pension scheme trust: DISP 2.7.9R (2).

and other financial institutions. They also include 'large undertakings' meeting two of the following requirements: (i) a balance sheet total of 20 million; (ii) net turnover of 40 million; or (iii) own funds of at least 2 million.[37] Bodies corporate that have share capital or net assets of at least £5 million are also caught. There are many more besides.[38]

Elective professional clients are clients that firms may treat as professional clients, provided they meet the criteria set out in COBS 3.5.3R. Those criteria are that:

1. The firm must assess their expertise with the result that this gives them reasonable assurance that the client can make their own investment decisions.

2. In connection with MiFID or equivalent third country business, the client must meet two of the following criteria: (i) the client has carried out transactions, in significant size, on the relevant market at an average frequency of 10 per quarter over the previous four quarters; (ii) the size of the client's financial instrument portfolio, defined as including cash deposits and financial instruments, exceeds 500,000; and (iii) the client works or has worked in the financial sector for at least one year in a professional position, which requires knowledge of the transactions or services envisaged.

3. The procedure for agreeing with the client that they are to be treated as a professional client has been complied with, including a statement in writing from the client that it wishes to be treated as a professional client; the provision of a clear written warning by the firm of the protections that the investor may lose; and a statement from the client that it is aware of the consequences of losing such protections.

Eligible counterparties are defined in COBS 3.6. They again come in two

---

[37] For MiFID or equivalent third-party business. Different limits apply for other business.

[38] They are listed in COBS 3.5.2R.

types: (i) *per se* eligible counterparties; and (ii) elective eligible counterparties. They will typically be larger institutions.

These exceptions were presumably designed to ensure that large and sophisticated institutions, and those that are themselves authorised by the FCA, cannot complain to the FOS. DISP 2.7.9AR provides that the exceptions above do not apply to a complainant who is a consumer in relation to the activity to which the complaint relates but given that only individuals can be consumers (see 'A consumer' above) this proviso is unlikely to apply very often.

A further exception applies to new complaints under transitional orders,[39] but this seems likely to be of historical interest only.

---

[39] DISP 2.7.10G.

CHAPTER SIX

TIME LIMITS FOR COMPLAINTS TO THE FOS

There are tight time limits for referring a complaint to the FOS. It is clear from the rules that the FOS is responsible for considering whether a dispute has been referred in time, and its decision will only be capable of review on the usual grounds for judicial review (see Chapter 17).

First, a FOS complaint should not be brought too early (although see below for circumstances in which the FOS will consider complaints 'early'). The FOS is intended to operate as a fallback if the firm has failed to resolve the complaint satisfactorily using its own complaint handling mechanisms.

Secondly, a FOS complaint can be dismissed if it is brought too late. There are two different events by reference to which it can be decided if the complainant is out of time. They are:

1. The final response issued by the relevant respondent[1] (though as we will see there is an exception for consumer redress schemes); or

2. The date of events in respect of which a complaint is made occurred[2].

As explained by Nugee LJ in *Shop Direct Finance Co v Official Receiver* [2023] EWCA Civ 367, the first of these issues is concerned about complaints being brought too early; the second is concerned with

1 See DISP 2.8.1R.

2 See DISP 2.8.2R.

complaints being brought too late.[3]

The respondent's final response

The FOS's procedures are supposed to act as an alternative to the respondent's own complaint handling procedures, which the respondent is required to have in place by DISP 1.

DISP 1 draws a distinction between MiFID complaints[4] (which are dealt with in DISP 1.1A) and other complaints. For most customers this is broadly irrelevant, but the effect is that provided that the rule in DISP 1.1A is marked with a 'UK',[5] as opposed to the usual 'R' or 'G', it will apply to complaints *to the respondent* from all clients who are not otherwise eligible complainants, and thus will include retail clients, professional clients and eligible counterparties. These rules do not impact on the question of whether a complaint can be brought before the FOS, which is governed by different parts of DISP.

DISP 1 requires the respondent to investigate complaints '*competently, diligently and impartially*' and to offer redress where it decides that it is appropriate.[6] As part of those procedures, the respondent is required to

---

3 See [131]-[132].

4 DISP 1.1A.3G: a MiFID complaint is one which concerns: (i) the provision of investment services or ancillary services to a client by an investment firm; (ii) the provision of investment services to a client by a CRD credit institution; (iii) the selling of structured deposits to clients or advising on these, when the sale or advice is provided by an investment firm or CRD credit institution; (iv) activities permitted by the UK provisions implementing Article 6(3) of the UCITS Directive carried on or by a Collective Portfolio Management Investment firm ('CPMI'); or (v) activities permitted by the UK provisions implementing under Article 6(4) of AIFMD when carried on or by a CPMI. A MiFID complaint is also a complaint about the equivalent business of a third country investment firm: DISP 1.1A.4G. The Glossary in the FCA Handbook defines this as '*the business of a third country investment firm carried on from an establishment in the United Kingdom that would be MiFID business if that firm were a MiFID investment firm.*'

5 Or is DISP 1.1A.39R which will also apply.

6 DISP 1.4.1R and DISP 1.1A.20R.

issue either a 'summary resolution communication'[7] or a 'final response'.[8] In practice, most complaints lead to a final response, and so for the remainder of this chapter we only refer to final responses.

In cases other than those relating to electronic money and payment services (so-called EMD or PSD complaints),[9] the final response should be issued by the respondent within eight weeks of receipt of the complaint and is a written response, which sets out the respondent's position on the complaint.

The respondent is required to enclose the FOS's explanatory leaflet and tell the complainant that, if they are dissatisfied with the resolution or response, they may be able to refer the complaint to the FOS. It should also include the FOS's website address. The respondent should also inform the complainant whether it (the respondent) will waive the time limits that apply to FOS claims (as discussed below) and, if not, it should refer explicitly to the time limits and the need to refer the complaint within them.[10]

If the respondent is unable to provide its final response within 8 weeks, then the respondent should set this out in a written response, but should also inform the complainant that they may now refer their complaint to the FOS.[11]

DISP 2.8.1R states that, unless the respondent consents, complainants may not refer their complaints to the FOS before either the final response has been provided or eight weeks have elapsed since the complainant complained and no final response has been forthcoming.[12]

---

7 DISP 1.5.4R.

8 DISP 1.6.2R.

9 As to which, see DISP 1.6.2A, requiring a final response within 15 business days or, exceptionally, 35 business days but only if a holding response has been sent within 15 business days.

10 DISP 1.6.2R.

11 DISP 1.6.2R(2).

12 Except for electronic money and payment services complaints, in which case the

Time limit from the final response

The final response is important in that, subject to the exceptions set out below, the FOS has no power to consider a complaint if it is referred to the FOS more than 6 months after the final response.[13]

DISP 2.8.3G refers to the need for a final response to refer to the six-month time limit. The implication is that a final response which fails to do so will not start time running.

Subsequent correspondence after the final response does not extend time, absent a formal and clear withdrawal of the final response.[14]

Consumer redress schemes

If the complaint was considered under a consumer redress scheme under section 404 or 404F(7) of FSMA, then there will be a 'redress determination' rather than a final response.[15] Such a complaint may only be referred after the redress determination has been issued, or should have been issued under the time limits specified by the scheme. The FOS has no jurisdiction to consider complaints raised more than six months after the redress determination.[16]

---

complaint can be referred after 15 business days if there has been no holding response, and after 35 business if there has been a holding response.

13 DISP 2.8.2R(1).

14 *R (Bankole) v FOS* [2012] EWHC 3555 (Admin) at [24].

15 A 'redress determination' is defined in the Glossary to the FCA Handbook as a written communication from a respondent under a consumer redress scheme that: (i) sets out the results of the respondent's determination under the scheme; (ii) encloses a copy of the FOS' standard explanatory leaflet; and (iii) informs the complainant that, if they are dissatisfied, they may now make a complaint to the FOS and must do so within six months.

16 DISP 2.8.2R (1).

Time limit from the events in respect of which a complaint is made

Subject to the exceptions set out below, the FOS also has no power to consider a complaint, if it is referred to the FOS after the later of:

1. Six years after the event complained of; or

2. Three years from the date on which the complainant became aware or ought reasonably to have become aware that they had cause for complaint.[17]

Shop Direct Finance Co v Official Receiver [2023] EWCA Civ 367 {'*Shop Direct*') considered the latter of these provisions in the context of the Official Receiver acting as trustee in bankruptcy for individuals who had purchased PPI. The question was whether the individual's knowledge was relevant, or the knowledge of the Official Receiver. The court rejected the argument that the Official Receiver's knowledge was all that mattered. It did not reach a firm conclusion on whose knowledge counted, but it seems likely that the three-year time period starts on the earlier of the customer's knowledge (pre-bankruptcy) and that of the Official Receiver.

These time limits apply unless, in either case, a complaint was made to the respondent or the FOS within the relevant period and there is written acknowledgment or record of the complaint having been received. This wording is important: it means that complaints can be referred to the FOS outside of the time limits, provided the complaint was referred to the respondent in time. In essence, the complaint to the respondent will stop time running, though the complainant will still need to refer their complaint within six months of receiving a final response from the respondent.

There is no general equivalent of the fifteen-year 'long-stop' date in the Limitation Act 1980 (though see below for the long-stop date for PPI claims).[18] In *R (Bamber) v FOS* [2009] EWCA Civ 593 the court rejected

17 DISP 2.8.2R (2).

18 S. 15B of that Act, in relation to negligence claims not involving personal injuries.

an argument that this was unlawful as abrogating the respondent's accrued rights under the 1980 Act.

Similarly, in *Shop Direct*, Singh LJ noted that the limitation provisions broadly mirror the law of limitation, but do not (as they could have done) use the same language.

In *Stuart Binns & Associates v FOS* [2021] EWHC 1620 (Admin), the court also rejected an argument that there was any obligation on the FOS to consider the ordinary law of limitation when applying its rules.[19] Accordingly, it seems clear that the FOS is not bound to apply its rules to ensure consistency with the law on limitation.

In certain cases delay might be relevant to what is 'fair and reasonable' in a case (see Chapter 11) even if it does not breach the time limits set out in DISP. Fordham J recognised this possibility in *Stuart Binns & Associates v FOS* [2021] EWHC 1620 (Admin), whilst rejecting the argument that the FOS had erred in failing to address delay on the facts of that case.[20]

R (Mortgage Agency Service Number Five) v FOS [2022] EWHC 1979 (Admin) raised the question of whether the FOS could consider matters that predate the relevant limitation period. The complainant complained about interest rates that had been charged on a mortgage over ten years. The FOS concluded that the complaint was limited to the most recent six years' payments, but also that it should consider changes to the interest charged prior to that period. The court upheld that approach.

Exception: the respondent consents

None of the time limits identified above apply where the respondent consents to the FOS considering the complaint even though the complaint has been brought late, except in relation to complaints under

---

19 See [16].

20 See [17].

consumer redress schemes.[21] Once a respondent has consented, it cannot withdraw that consent.[22]

As part of UK's implementation of Directive 2013/11/EU concerning alternative dispute resolution for consumer disputes, the DISP 2 rules relating to complaint referrals to the FOS were amended to enable FOS to consider complaints 'early' – namely, before the respondent has investigated a complaint.

Under DISP 2.8.1R(4), the FOS can consider the complaint before the respondent has investigated it provided that the respondent consents; the FOS has informed the complainant that the respondent must deal with the complaint within eight weeks and that it may resolve the complaint more quickly than the FOS;[23] and the complainant nevertheless wishes the FOS to deal with the complaint.

Exception: exceptional circumstances

The time limits do not apply if there has been a failure to comply because of 'exceptional circumstances'.[24] DISP 2.8.4G gives the example of a complainant having been incapacitated.

The FOS's website provides further guidance on this exception,[25] which suggest that serious ill health may suffice, if the FOS is persuaded that the complainant delayed their complaint because of their treatment or because they were dealing with a family bereavement. The FOS website used to give further examples including complainants caring for relatives abroad for an extended period, such that they do not see the final response. Following the deletion of 'technical notes' from the FOS

21 DISP 2.8.2R (5).

22 DISP 2.8.2AR.

23 Or 15 business days for EMD or PSD complaints or, in exceptional circumstances, 35 business days.

24 DISP 2.8.2R(3).

25 https://www.financial-ombudsman.org.uk/consumers/expect/time-limits.

website (though they can still be viewed in online archives[26]), it is unclear whether this example would still be persuasive.

Those same FOS technical notes suggested that it would not extend time because complainants had previously believed that they had little prospect of success, or because of illnesses that did not prevent the complainant from corresponding with the respondent. Likewise, being busy at work or being made redundant was not thought of as 'exceptional'.

It seems that the FOS is not required to consider of its own motion whether this exception applies. However, in some cases it would be sensible for the FOS specifically to address the issue to avoid unfairness or confusion and where that is so may have to raise the point itself.[27]

Exception: transitional arrangements

The usual time limits do not apply if the FOS is required under transitional arrangements to hear the complaint.[28]

Exception: pension transfers etc.

The six- and three-year time limits do not apply if the complaint concerns a contract or policy which is or was under review under the policies issued by the FSA in relation to pension transfers and opt outs and FSAVC (i.e. a voluntary contribution arrangement in connection with certain types of occupational pension schemes) on 25 October 1994 and 28 February 2000 respectively.[29]

Likewise, provisions exist in relation to the sale of mortgage endowment

---

26 https://web.archive.org/web/20180830115335/http://www.financial-ombudsman.org.uk/publications/technical_notes/six-month-time-limit.htm.

27 *R (Bankole) v FOS* [2012] EWHC 3555 (Admin) at [15] and [24].

28 DISP 2.8.2R and the FSMA 2000 (Transitional provisions) (Ombudsman Scheme and Complaints Scheme) Order 2001.

29 DISP 2.8.5R.

policies to ensure that time for referring a complaint does not run until the complainant has been told that there is a high risk the policy will not produce a large enough sum to repay the mortgage at maturity.[30] Note that the requirement is for the complainant to be told there is a 'high risk'. Being told of the fact there was 'a risk' is not enough. Time will end three years after the relevant letter, provided that the complainant is told, at least six months before the final date to refer the complainant, that the time to refer the complaint will expire at that date.[31]

The final exception relates to PPI complaints. Because of the widespread publicity about the sale of PPI, DISP 2.8.8G clarifies that mere knowledge that there was a problem with the sale of PPI 'generally' is not normally enough to start the three-year time limit running to bring a complaint relating to a failure to disclose commission.[32]

The FOS has also imposed a long stop date on PPI claims. If the sale occurred before 29 August 2017 and the complaint expresses dissatisfaction about the sale, the complaint was required to be referred to the FOS before 29 August 2019,[33] though this is not so if a failure to comply with that long stop date occurs due to exceptional circumstances.[34] The respondent may also consent to the complaint being heard out of time.[35] Finally, if the PPI contract was live after 29 August 2019, and was rejected on the grounds of ineligibility exclusion or limitation, then complaints relating to the grounds of rejection can be made after 29 August 2019.[36]

30 DISP 2.8.6G.

31 DISP 2.8.7R(2). Time will instead run until a date specified in the explanation, which cannot be less than 6 months (DISP 2.8.7R(4)).

32 See DISP App 3.3A.2E.

33 DISP 2.8.9R (2)(a).

34 DISP 2.8.2R (3).

35 DISP 2.8.9R (2)(c).

36 DISP 2.8.2R (2)(d).

CHAPTER SEVEN

PROCEDURE: AN INTRODUCTION

This book will now consider the procedural steps of a FOS decision, from the FOS's receipt of a complaint through to an ombudsman's final decision.[1]

In these chapters we do not address the tests that that the FOS will apply to resolve the complaint: those issues are discussed in chapter 11. However, it is impossible to divorce the two issues entirely. The FOS is to determine complaints by reference to what is 'fair and reasonable', and the same test is relevant to the procedure adopted by the FOS, as we shall see below when considering the availability of oral hearings.

The starting point for the FOS's procedure is FSMA, s. 225(1): the FOS was set up so that '*certain disputes may be resolved quickly and with minimum formality by an independent person*'.

Consistent with this, the FOS is entitled to take a very different approach from a court of law.[2] In summary:

1. The FOS is inquisitorial rather than adversarial.

2. Oral hearings are the exception rather than the rule: the FOS will typically resolve a complaint based on written evidence and

---

1 There are circumstances in which the FOS will need to apply the rules of a former scheme: DISP 3.1.4G. Such former scheme rules are outside the ambit of this chapter.

2 Emphasised in *R (Heather Moor & Edgecomb) v FOS* [2009] EWHC 2701 (Admin) at [8]. As the FOS state on their website: '... *the decision we come to on what is fair and reasonable in all the circumstances of the case may be different to what a court would decide applying legal rules*': https://www.financial-ombudsman.org.uk/who-we-are/make-decisions.

arguments.

3. The strict rules of evidence do not apply to the FOS.

Nevertheless, the FOS is a tribunal for the purpose of Article 6 of the European Convention on Human Rights,[3] and so its procedures should comply with the requirements of that Article and should be concluded within a reasonable time.

The use of lawyers and claims management companies

Both complainants and respondents can use lawyers to represent them in relation to FOS complaints, and this is quite normal for larger disputes. The FOS, however, takes the view that such assistance is not necessary, and *'you generally don't need anyone to represent you'*.[4]

It is also very common for complaints to be pursued by claims management companies on behalf of consumers.

The FOS recently noted that, across all categories of complaints, there has been an increase in complaints brought by claims management companies and other professional representations: 25% of cases in 2023/24, up from 18% in 2022/23.[5] In recognition of the significant involvement of claims management companies and other professional representatives in bringing complaints on behalf of consumers, the FOS has proposed charging up to £250 as a case fee. The fee would be reduced to £75 if the case outcome is in favour of the consumer.[6]

---

3 *R (Calland) v FOS* [2013] EWHC 1327 (Admin) at [35].

4 https://www.financial-ombudsman.org.uk/who-we-are/make-decisions.

5 https://www.financial-ombudsman.org.uk/data-insight/annual-complaints-data/annual-complaints-data-insight-2023-24.

6 https://www.financial-ombudsman.org.uk/news/charges-professional-representatives-detailed-first-time-new-ombudsman-service-consultation. As at the date of publication, the proposed charge has not been introduced.

The role of investigators and ombudsmen

In this book, we regularly refer to the FOS as though it was the body making the decisions. This is used as shorthand, as FOS decisions are reached by ombudsmen, and a decision reached by an ombudsman is the final stage in resolving a complaint.

The DISP rules only talk about ombudsmen (not the FOS) and they also omit any reference to the investigation stage of FOS complaints.

In fact, many FOS complaints never reach ombudsmen and are dealt with by investigators[7] (sometimes referred to as 'adjudicators'). Investigators undertake initial fact finding in relation to the complaint, and in a typical case they will produce their assessment of the complaint, complete with an assessment of the appropriate redress (if any). In essence, this is a preliminary decision, which either party can reject and escalate the complaint to an ombudsman for a final decision.

For example, an investigator may seek facts from both parties before concluding that the complaint should lead to some form of compensation. If both parties accept that recommendation, then they will settle the complaint based on the investigator's view. If either party does not wish to accept the recommendation, the complaint will be referred to an ombudsman.

Although they do not feature in the rules, these assessments by investigators are the endpoint for most FOS complaints. Only about 14% of complaints are resolved by ombudsmen.[8]

If a complaint is referred to an ombudsman, they will consider the investigator's findings but are expected to form their own view of the facts, and may require further information from the parties, before issuing their decision (set out below). Even once the matter has been referred to an ombudsman, the investigator will remain involved as the

7 In a rare acknowledgment of this stage of the process, see *R (Linear Investments Ltd) v FOS* [2024] EWHC 1428 (Admin).

8 The FOS Annual Review 2022/23 showed that, of the 209,471 complaints resolved, 29,854 reached a final decision by an ombudsman.

parties' main point of contact.

There is a large panel of ombudsmen, appointed as individuals of '*appropriate qualifications and experience*'.[9] There is no jurisdictional limit on an ombudsman considering any kind of complaint.

A list of ombudsmen can be found on the FOS's website, which provides limited CVs for each of them.[10] A review of that list suggests that a great many of them have risen through the FOS, from investigator to ombudsman.

From the panel of ombudsmen, a Chief Ombudsman is appointed.[11] The Chief Ombudsman represents the FOS to the outside world but has no special powers in relation to FOS complaints.

Timescales

Under the relevant regulations, complaints are supposed to be dealt with within 90 days save in 'highly complex disputes'.[12]

The FOS's Annual Report and Accounts for 2022/2023 stated that median waiting time was down from 6.4 months in 2021/22 to 4.8 months in 2022/23. The FOS's 2024/25 Plans and Budget refers to a target to resolve 90% of cases from 'conversion' within 6 months.

In our experience, few disputed complaints that go all the way to a final decision are resolved within 90 days.

---

9 FSMA, Schedule 17, Part II, para 4.

10 https://www.financial-ombudsman.org.uk/who-we-are/staff/ombudsmen.

11 FSMA, Schedule 17, Part II, para 5.

12 Originally Directive 2013/11/EU, Article 8(e). In the UK, this provision was implemented under paragraph 6(d), Schedule 3 to the Alternative Dispute Resolution for Consumer Disputes (Competent Authorities and Information) Regulations 2015. These regulations are due to be revoked by the Digital Markets, Competition and Consumers Act 2024, under which the FOS will be exempt from the replacement provisions: s. 295 and Sch 25 Part 2.

Despite the regulations referred to above, the FOS does not have a set time limit in which it is required to resolve a complaint. There have been unusual examples of complaints that took 5 years to resolve.[13]

The length of time that the complaint takes will depend upon the stage that it reaches: a complaint resolved by accepting an investigator's findings will generally be quicker than a complaint with a dispute about jurisdiction, followed by provisional and final decisions from an ombudsman.

13 *R (Green) v FOS* [2012] EWHC 1253 (Admin). In *Options UK Personal Pensions v FOS* [2024] EWCA Civ 541 the decision took 4½ years (from November 2017 to March 2022), and the judicial review proceedings took another 2 years (May 2024).

CHAPTER EIGHT

DETERMINING JURISDICTION AND SUMMARY DISMISSAL OF COMPLAINTS

This chapter deals with three situations in which a complaint can be disposed of without a final decision on the merits because:

1. The complaint is out of the FOS's jurisdiction.
2. The complaint is dismissed summarily for one of several reasons enumerated below.
3. The dispute is referred to another complaints scheme, or the court.

Determining jurisdiction

In the initial stages, the FOS will consider whether the complaint is within its jurisdiction. In most cases, this is likely to be a formality, and there will be no need for representations or a formal decision by an ombudsman.

In other cases, particularly where time limits appear to be in issue, it is likely that the FOS will want to investigate whether it has jurisdiction to determine the complaint. The jurisdiction question therefore can become a substantial stage of the FOS processes.[1] The respondent can also require the FOS to reach a decision if it disputes jurisdiction on a complaint. When it does so, the FOS will then give both parties the chance to make

---

1 DISP 3.2.4R provides that, when the Ombudsman considers that the complaint may be out of jurisdiction, he will give the complainant an opportunity to make representations before he decides.

representations.[2] Likewise, the FOS may take it upon itself to consider jurisdiction where it considers that the complaint might be outside of its jurisdiction.[3]

In practice, in such cases it will usually be an investigator who gathers evidence and expresses a view before the ombudsman produces a provisional decision and then a final decision on jurisdiction.

In one extreme example, a complaint was initiated in July 2005, and the respondent vigorously objected to jurisdiction. After delays that were largely due to the respondent itself, jurisdiction was not resolved until October 2009.[4]

If the FOS does not have jurisdiction, then the complaint will not proceed.[5] A complainant unhappy with this conclusion would need to consider judicial review proceedings at this stage (see Chapter 17).

If the FOS concludes that it does have jurisdiction, then the complaint will continue. The FOS's stated position in court has been that it will continue to consider whether it has jurisdiction until the final decision on the merits,[6] and on occasion has been persuaded to reopen the question of jurisdiction even after issuing a decision.[7] A respondent that is unhappy with the outcome on jurisdiction appears therefore to have a choice whether to commence judicial review proceedings at this point, or after the final decision on the merits. For more detail on this issue see Chapter 17.

---

2 DISP 3.2.3R.

3 Ibid.

4 See *R (Calland) v FOS* [2013] EWHC 1327 (Admin) at [41]–[66].

5 DISP 3.2.5R provides that where the Ombudsman decides that the complaint is out of jurisdiction, he will give reasons for that decision to the complainant and inform the respondent.

6 *R (Chancery (UK) LLP) v FOS* [2015] EWHC 407 (Admin) at [78].

7 See *R (iDealing.com) v FOS* [2024] EWHC 847 (Admin) at [38].

Dismissal of complaints without consideration

In addition to the possibility of a complaint being out of jurisdiction, DISP 3.3.4AR sets out the current rules[8] for dismissing a complaint without consideration of the merits. The FOS 'may' dismiss complaints on five grounds, which are set out below. Previously, the rules stated that the FOS 'must' consider whether to dismiss a case summarily. As the wording of the rules has changed, we consider that comments in cases suggesting an obligation on the FOS to consider dismissal probably no longer represent the law.[9]

If the FOS is considering dismissing a complaint on one of these grounds, then the complainant will be given an opportunity to make representations.[10]

The decision whether to dismiss a complaint summarily may be delegated to a designated member of staff.[11]

Although, typically, complaints are dismissed under these rules early in the process, there is nothing to stop the FOS from dismissing complaints at any time.[12] It may be the case, for example, that evidence emerges late in the day to show that the complaint is frivolous or vexatious. Instead of proceeding to a final decision, the ombudsman could choose to dismiss the complaint.

---

8 DISP 3.3.4R sets out the rules for complaints referred to the FOS before 9 July 2015, which is now only of historical interest.

9 *R (Heather Moor & Edgecomb) v FOS* [2008] EWCA Civ 643 at [35]–[36].

10 DISP 3.3.1R.

11 *R (Heather Moor & Edgecomb) v FOS* [2008] EWCA Civ 643 at [47].

12 There is nothing in DISP 3.3 to limit the time at which the powers can be used and the ability of the FOS to dismiss complaints 'at any stage' is stated in the Glossary definition of 'Chargeable Case'.

Frivolous or vexatious complaints

The FOS may summarily dismiss a complaint if it considers that the complaint is 'frivolous or vexatious'.[13]

2.3% of cases dismissed between July 2022 and July 2023 were dismissed on this basis.[14]

The FOS does not provide guidance on what will be seen as frivolous or vexatious.[15] However, it seems to us that the following types of complaint may qualify as frivolous or vexatious:

1. Where the complainant has not been inconvenienced and will suffer no loss as a result of the actions complained about.

2. Very regular complaints from the same complainant about the same respondent, in relation to minor matters, such that the effect is to harass the respondent.

3. Complaints which have the clear intention of harassing the respondent by reason of the respondent's obligation to pay case fees irrespective of the outcome (see Chapter 12).

4. Claims with no basis at all, such as cases where the FOS found that no PPI policy existed at all for the relevant person.[16]

It is unclear whether a complaint without any reasonable prospects of success could be said to be vexatious on that ground alone (i.e. where there is no doubt that financial services were provided, but the FOS

---

13 DISP 3.3.4A(1).

14 FOS, 'Alternative Dispute Resolution Annual Activity Report 2022/2023'. A total of 4,048 cases were dismissed during this period of which 92 were on the basis of the complaint being frivolous and vexatious.

15 In response to a Freedom of Information request, the FOS stated in 2014 that its 'Knowledge and Information Toolkit' does not include notes on frivolous or vexatious complaints: https://ico.org.uk/media/action-weve-taken/decision-notices/2014/1008586/fs_50500980.pdf.

16 As referred to in the FOS's 'Annual Activity Report 2016/2017'.

immediately concludes that the respondent did nothing wrong). For complaints prior to 9 July 2015, that was an independent ground for dismissing a claim,[17] but it was deleted for later complaints.

The DISP rules do not provide for the respondent making representations in respect of summary dismissal, but it is easy to think of examples where it would be appropriate for the respondent to make such submissions. For example, if the complainant had indicated to the respondent that a complaint would be made as a form of blackmail (knowing that a case fee would be payable by the respondent), then the respondent should be entitled to provide evidence of that fact to the FOS.

<u>Complaint dealt with by a comparable ADR entity</u>

If a complaint has already been dealt with by a comparable 'ADR entity', then the claim may be dismissed.[18]

This ground for dismissing a claim was based on a European Directive,[19] and is for the time being is based on the ADR Regulations.[20] There does not appear to be any mechanism for the FOS to find out about previous decisions by another ADR entity, unless a Respondent relies on this ground.

The FOS's statistics suggest that 44 complaints were dismissed on this basis in 2022/2023.[21]

---

17 DISP 3.3.4R.

18 DISP 3.3.4A (2).

19 Directive 2013/11/EU.

20 Alternative Dispute Resolution for Consumer Disputes (Competent Authorities and Information) Regulations 2015. These regulations are due to be revoked by the Digital Markets, Competition and Consumers Act 2024, under which the FOS will be exempt from the replacement provisions: s. 295 and Sch 25 Part 2.

21 'Annual Activity Report for 2022/2023'. This amounted to 1.1% of the 4,048 dismissed claims in this period.

Matters subject to litigation

Where a court has already ruled upon the merits of a dispute, the FOS has the power to dismiss the claim.[22] Whilst it is acceptable for a complainant to attempt a FOS complaint first, before turning to litigation, it is generally not acceptable to go through the court process and then complain to the FOS and it would be a rare case that the FOS was willing to consider despite the court having given a decision on the merits.

According to the FOS's Annual Activity Report for 2022/2023, 65 complaints were dismissed on this basis.[23]

Court proceedings currently under way

The FOS may also refuse to consider a complaint if court proceedings are on foot and have not been stayed for consideration by the FOS.[24] We consider this situation from the perspective of the court proceeding in Chapter 16. It is up to the parties or the court whether to stay court proceedings but, if they are not stayed, then the FOS may dismiss the complaint.

According to the FOS's Annual Activity Report for 2022/2023, 41 complaints were dismissed on this basis.[25]

An attempt was made in *R (Westcott Financial Services Ltd) v FOS* [2014] EWHC 3972 (Admin) ('*Westcott*') to argue that the FOS should also stay complaints where similar court proceedings were under way. Importantly, the relevant court proceedings did not involve the specific complainants, and were effectively test cases of similar but not identical facts. The FOS refused to stay the claims, and this approach was upheld

22 DISP 3.3.4AR (3).

23 Annual Activity Report for 2022/2023. This amounted to 1.6% of the 4,048 dismissed claims in this period.

24 DISP 3.3.4AR (4).

25 Amounting to 1% of the 4,048 dismissed claims in this period.

by the court.

On the other hand, in the context of court proceedings, disciplinary proceedings and other enquiries, the FOS indicated in 2005 that it was not willing to consider particular types of complaints in relation to Equitable Life (discussed below).[26]

It may be questioned whether the FOS would have had the ability, let alone the obligation, to stay proceedings because of parallel court proceedings involving other parties. The DISP rules only refer to dismissal of the complaints where the subject matter of the complaints has been or is the subject of court proceedings but, as the complainants in *Westcott* were not parties to any court action, the rule was inapplicable. No other rule is cited in *Westcott* as a basis for the staying the complaints.

Impairment of the operation of the FOS

The final ground on which a complaint can be dismissed is where it would '*seriously impair the effective operation*' of the FOS.[27] This appears to be something of a catch-all for other complaints that the FOS dismisses without consideration of the merits. Importantly, though, a deluge of complaints in a particular area does not appear to be sufficient to prevent the FOS considering such complaints under this rule. The FOS is well used to dealing with widespread complaints, and in appropriate cases has set up bespoke procedures to address them.

This criterion is expanded upon by DISP 3.3.4BG, which lists several specific situations where complaints may be dismissed, considered in turn below.

According to the FOS's Annual Activity Report for 2022/2023, 3,806 complaints were dismissed under this heading, amounting to the overwhelming majority (94%) of total dismissed claims for this period.

---

26 https://web.archive.org/web/20150608030054/http://www.financial-ombudsman.org.uk/faq/pdf/Equitable_Penrose-related_decision.pdf

27 DISP 3.3.4AR (4).

Complaint better dealt with by a court

The FOS may dismiss a case if it considers that it is more appropriate for a court or a comparable ADR entity.[28] This should be distinguished from the FOS's ability to refer test cases to the court or other ADR entities (discussed in Chapter 16) though the two issues are obviously closely linked.

Some guidance on the FOS's approach to this rule may be gleaned from its decision dated 22 March 2005 in relation to various complaints that relied upon findings made by Lord Penrose in respect of Equitable Life products. [29] The FOS decided that it was not an appropriate forum to determine such complaints, noting that there was a possibility of 'stalemate' if FOS decisions overlapped with the FSA's regulatory powers or the decisions were challenged. In the setting of other court and disciplinary proceedings currently underway, and potentially wide implications of any FOS decision on the issues, the FOS decided that it would be more suitable for the complaints to be dealt with by a court.

In *R (Chancery Tax (UK) LLP) v FOS* [2015] EWHC 407 (Admin), the court referred to a final decision in which it was said that the FOS does not usually dismiss cases purely based on the amount in dispute.[30]

From experience, a factor that the FOS may consider is the fact that the complaint includes allegations of fraud, or other difficult issues which require cross-examination in court. Although the FOS has jurisdiction to allow oral hearings (see Chapter 10), some cases can only fairly be resolved under oath and with full disclosure from both parties.

---

28 DISP 3.3.4BG(1).

29 https://web.archive.org/web/20150608030054/http://www.financial-ombudsman.org.uk/faq/pdf/Equitable_Penrose-related_decision.pdf.

30 At [44].

Complaint previously determined

A complaint may be dismissed on the basis that the FOS has already considered it or excluded it, unless '*material new evidence to affect the outcome has subsequently become available*'.[31] Accordingly, this provision applies where the FOS has previously decided the complaint, and it allows the FOS to reconsider the complaint again.

R (Cook) v FOS [2009] EWHC 426 (Admin), relied on the test set out in *Ladd v Marshall* [1954] 1 WLR 1489 applicable in civil appeals, as the basis for concluding that evidence should only be treated as new if it could not with reasonable diligence have been obtained at the time of the original complaint.[32] On the facts of that case, the complainants sought to rely on an expert report as new evidence, but the court agreed with the FOS's position that the complainants could have obtained that report at the time of the original complaint.

However, in *R (Moniak) v FOS* [2023] EWHC 333 (Admin), the court concluded that the *Ladd v Marshall* test had no direct application. The reasons for not obtaining evidence earlier was, no doubt, part of the evaluative judgment to be reached by the FOS but it is not itself determinative.[33] In that case, the FOS was found to have acted irrationally in refusing to consider transcripts of court proceedings, which contradicted a note of the hearing that the firm had previously relied upon, on a key matter in dispute.

The cases above leave open a question: where the previous complaint led to a final decision, accepted by the complainants, can the FOS reconsider the complaint based on new evidence? This might occur where the FOS upholds a complaint and calculates losses on a particular basis. The later evidence might demonstrate that the complainant had suffered larger losses. Given that such a final decision becomes binding on both the complainant and the respondent, the FOS's position in *Cook* was that the

31 DISP 3.3.4A(5) and 3.3.4BG(3).

32 At [35]–[37].

33 See [66].

complaint could not be reconsidered.

Referring disputes to other complaints schemes or the court

The rules provide for the FOS to refer complaints elsewhere in only two circumstances.

The first circumstance is that the FOS considers that another complaints scheme might be more suitable, and the complainant consents to the referral.[34]

For example, a complainant might be making a complaint about their pension arrangements, and it is possible that the Pensions Ombudsman might be more suitable. In fact, the FOS agreed a memorandum of understanding with the Pensions Ombudsman[35], which explains that the issues that each service will consider when deciding whether to refer a complaint to the other include:

1. The potential redress and the limits applicable to each service, if the other service can make greater awards.
2. The applicable time limits for each service, such that a complaint might be out of time with the FOS but in time for the Pensions Ombudsman.
3. If a complaint relates to multiple respondents and the FOS only has jurisdiction over one respondent whereas the Pensions Ombudsman has jurisdiction over both respondents.

If a complainant refuses the transfer, the memorandum of understanding suggests that the FOS might decide to dismiss the complaint in accordance with its usual powers. In other words, it may dismiss the complaint under the rules described above.

34 DISP 3.4.1R.

35 https://www.financial-ombudsman.org.uk/files/2629/memorandum_of_understanding-with-Pensions-Ombudsman-December-2017.pdf.

Though it is not apparent in the rules, the FOS may also refer complaints to the Pensions Ombudsman even without the complainant's consent, if the FOS concludes that it does not have jurisdiction but that the Pensions Ombudsman might be able to consider the complaint.[36]

The second circumstance in which the FOS will consider referring a case is where the complaint could usefully be considered by the courts as a test case. Again, this can only happen with the complainant's consent. We consider this in greater detail in Chapter 16.[37]

---

[36] Pursuant to the memorandum of understanding dated 1 December 2017 available at: https://www.financial-ombudsman.org.uk/files/2629/memorandum_of_understanding-with-Pensions-Ombudsman-December-2017.pdf.

[37] DISP 3.4.2R. Further guidance on the factors that the FOS will take into account are at DISP 3.4.3G.

CHAPTER NINE

FACT FINDING

The rules state that an ombudsman will give both parties an opportunity to make representations before proceeding to a decision.[1] In reality, much of the fact finding is conducted by investigators, before being considered by ombudsmen.

Typically, the FOS will contact the parties and seek information on specific issues. This is often by email and is an iterative process: the FOS may make repeated requests for evidence and seek explanations of issues that arise from that evidence. The FOS is entitled to look beyond the complaint itself and to look more widely at the available evidence.[2]

The FOS is not limited in the type of evidence it can consider. Unlike litigation, there are no 'rules of evidence' and the rules states explicitly that the FOS may exclude evidence that a court would accept or include evidence that would not be admissible in court.[3]

This means that there is no need for oaths, or formal witness statements, and the FOS will accept evidence provided by email or by any reasonable means.

Nevertheless, any party to a FOS complaint should do their best to provide contemporaneous documentary evidence to support their case. Particularly given the extreme rarity of oral hearings (see Chapter 10), the FOS will often accept such documents and written evidence at face value.

---

1 DISP 3.5.4R.

2 *R (Full Circle Asset Management Ltd) v FOS* [2017] EWHC 323 (Admin) at [54].

3 DISP 3.5.9R(1).

Expert evidence

Parties can put forward expert evidence in support of their case, but that is the exception rather than the norm. The FOS will not necessarily accept such evidence and may conclude that the respondent acted negligently even if the respondent obtains an expert report supporting its conduct.[4] If a party does wish to rely on an expert's report, however, it must do so before the final decision is issued. Attempts to do so at a later date will likely be too late.[5]

Likewise, a respondent can put forward an opinion from counsel[6] but the FOS is not bound to agree with it and can, in any event, reach a conclusion that is fair and reasonable, and contrary to the strict legal position (see Chapter 11).

Communications from the FOS

The FOS may also communicate with parties in a way that would not be appropriate by a judge in litigation. For example, there is no problem with the FOS enquiring with a respondent whether it intends to rely on a time-bar where the respondent has not raised the issue itself.[7]

The rules also allow the FOS to receive information on a confidential basis, so that it is not disclosed to the other party, or only in redacted form.[8] Whilst that may well be appropriate for some evidence, there may be issues with this approach if the information is crucial to the FOS's decision and is not disclosed. As we discuss in Chapter 17, the FOS is required to comply with the rules of natural justice, and this will typically require a party to understand and be able to respond to the evidence

---

4 *R (Heather Moor & Edgecomb) v FOS* [2008] EWCA Civ 642 at [56].

5 See *R (Cook) v FOS* [2009] EWHC 426 (Admin) and *R (Walker) v FOS* [2013] NIQB 12 at [22].

6 As in *R (IFG Financial Services Ltd) v FOS* [2005] EWHC 1153 (Admin).

7 *R (Ropaigealach) v FOS* [2005] EWCA Civ 269 at [15].

8 DISP 3.5.9R(2).

relied upon by the FOS.

Directions from the FOS

The FOS will usually set down time limits for the provision of evidence,[9] and a failure by a complainant to provide the evidence in time can lead to the FOS treating the complaint as withdrawn.[10] However, the FOS is often amenable to requests for more time to provide information, and it would be surprising for a single failure to meet a deadline to lead to such a result.

The FOS also has the power, under s. 231 of FSMA, to require either party to a complaint to provide information and documents. If that party does not provide the documents, then under s. 232 of FSMA the FOS may certify that fact to the High Court, and the party can be held in contempt of court if there is no reasonable excuse for withholding the information/documents. There are no reported cases in which the FOS has taken this step, and it is likely that it would only do so in extreme cases.

Particularly where it is the respondent that fails to provide information, it is more likely that the FOS would draw inferences from the lack of evidence and reach negative findings.[11] Given that respondents also have a duty to co-operate with the FOS,[12] there may also be regulatory consequences for refusing to provide information when requested.

The FOS's inquisitorial approach

Where the evidence suggests that the complaint has been formulated incorrectly, or misses the real problem, the FOS may consider a different formulation of the complaint. The FOS may also consider further

9 DISP 3.5.13R.

10 DISP 3.5.9R(4) and DISP 3.5.15R.

11 DISP 3.5.9R(4).

12 DISP 1.4.4R.

evidence, not provided by the parties. However, if it does so, the FOS should make it clear to both parties before reaching a final decision. In practice, this will normally be achieved through the provision of the investigator's findings and the ombudsman's provisional decision.[13]

Provisional and final decisions

Before an ombudsman issues a final decision, the rules require that both parties be sent a provisional decision.[14]

They are, as the name suggests, an expression by the ombudsman of factual findings, and the decision, that the ombudsman proposes to make. Provisional decisions are provided to the parties for comment, and often lead to further evidence or submissions by one party or the other, aimed at correcting what they see as the ombudsman's mistakes. Accordingly, the provisional decision should be seen as part of the fact-finding process, ensuring that the parties have an opportunity to make submissions on the ombudsman's proposed approach.

They also serve a protective purpose for the FOS: because the parties can see what the ombudsman is thinking, and what they are considering, it is hard to argue in a judicial review that either party was unaware of the case that they were expected to meet, prior to the final decision. This is discussed in Chapter 17.

The final decision should be supported by sufficient reasons that the parties can understand why the ombudsman reached his/her conclusions. However, the requirement is not as high as it would be for a judgment in court. Given the informal nature of FOS complaints, it will be sufficient if the ombudsman approaches matters on a common sense basis, and it is not required to address every argument put forward by the parties, as

13 See *R (Green) v FOS* [2003] EWHC 338 (Admin) at [49-52] and *R (Full Circle Asset Management) v FOS* [2017] EWHC 323 (Admin) at [57].

14 DISP 3.5.4R refers to 'provisional assessment', but they are more normally referred to as provisional decisions.

long as the conclusion is clear.[15]

As to the awards that the FOS may make, see Chapter 13.

15 *R (Garrison Investment Analysis) v FOS* [2006] EWHC 2466 (Admin) at [5].

CHAPTER TEN

ORAL HEARINGS

The current DISP rules relating to oral hearings state:

> *'If the Ombudsman considers that the complaint can be fairly determined without convening a hearing, he will determine the complaint. If not, he will invite the parties to take part in a hearing. A hearing may be held by any means which the Ombudsman considers appropriate in the circumstances, including by telephone. No hearing will be held after the Ombudsman has determined the complaint. ...*
>
> *In deciding whether there should be a hearing and, if so, whether it should be in public or private, the Ombudsman will have regard to the provisions of the European Convention on Human Rights.'*[1]

The circumstances relevant to whether the FOS should hold oral hearings have been considered several times by the courts, from which we draw the following propositions:

1. The European Convention on Human Rights does not contain an absolute right to an oral hearing: the overarching principle is one of fairness.[2]

2. Nevertheless, there may be cases in which fairness demands that an oral hearing take place.[3]

3. Where the fair determination of the complaint requires investigation of what was said at meetings, and those facts are

1 DISP 3.5.5R and DISP 3.5.7G.

2 *Jussila v Finland* (2006) 45 EHRR 892, quoted in *R (Heather Moor & Edgecomb) v FOS* [2008] EWCA Civ 642 at [64].

3 *R (Heather Moor & Edgecomb) v FOS* [2009] EWHC 2701 (Admin) at [10].

contested, fairness may require an oral hearing.[4] Even then, it may be sufficient to test the accuracy of the complainant's evidence in writing in the interests of efficiency and economy.[5]

4. The FOS is entitled to take a common-sense view of matters such as causation without hearing evidence from the complainant. For example, there will usually be no need for an oral hearing to test whether a complainant relied upon advice received from a financial advisor: it will usually be fair to presume reliance.[6]

5. Likewise, if the FOS takes the view that bad advice was given, then it will not be necessary to investigate precisely what was said as part of that bad advice.[7]

6. The FOS is also entitled to conclude that an oral hearing is unlikely to resolve disputed issues of fact, where the oral hearing would take place so long after the relevant meeting that it is unlikely to produce useful evidence.[8]

As a more general point, it should be noted there is no reported decision in which a FOS decision has been quashed by reason of the lack of an oral hearing. In *Options UK Personal Pensions LLP v FOS* [2024] EWCA Civ 541 the court recognised that '*[t]here can be no doubt, that the Ombudsman in this case, and the FOS in general, is not required to determine a complaint in accordance with the common law…*' and '*…the ombudsman service is intended to provide a quick and informal means of*

---

4 *R (Heather Moor & Edgecomb) v FOS* [2008] EWCA Civ 642 at [58].

5 *R (Heather Moor & Edgecomb) v FOS* [2008] EWCA Civ 642 at [65]. See also *Options UK Personal Pensions LLP v FOS* [2024] EWCA Civ 541 at [58].

6 *R (Heather Moor & Edgecomb) v FOS* [2008] EWCA Civ 642 at [60].

7 *R (Heather Moor & Edgecomb) v FOS* [2009] EWHC 2701 (Admin) at [13]. Similar reasoning was used in *R (Calland) v FOS* [2013] EWHC 1327 (Admin) at [113], where an advisor disputed the alleged advice he had given, but it was common ground that he had in fact given advice.

8 *R (Calland) v FOS* [2013] EWHC 1327 (Admin) at [114].

resolving certain disputes.'[9]

In preparation for the first edition of this book, the authors searched for the phrase 'oral hearing' on the database of FOS decisions. Out of 55 decisions listed, it appeared that no hearing had been held: in each case, the ombudsman reported that a hearing had been requested or at least mentioned by one of the parties, but none were held. Searching for the same phrase now produces over 400 results. A review of the most recent 10 results continues to suggest that requests for an oral hearing are very likely to be rejected, with the FOS relying on the case law we cite above.

Despite their apparent rarity, the FOS did produce 'a quick guide to hearings', which set out the approach that it would take to hearings. That guide is no longer available on the FOS website,[10] but in any event it provided little concrete guidance as to the type of situation in which a hearing will be held, beyond situations where '*we think a hearing will help resolve issues that are relevant.*'

The document suggested that, if a hearing were held:

1. It would occur after the investigator had issued their recommendations and before the ombudsman issued a final decision.

2. It would usually take place in the FOS's offices in London.

3. Questions would be put by the ombudsman. Direct cross-examination by one party of another is unlikely to be allowed. This has regularly been emphasised in recent decisions rejecting an oral hearing.[11]

4. Lawyers are discouraged, and if a respondent intends to attend with its legal representatives, the FOS might invite the

---

9 See [73].

10 https://web.archive.org/web/20170205161537/http://www.financial-ombudsman.org.uk/publications/technical_notes/QG3-hearings.pdf.

11 For example, see https://www.financial-ombudsman.org.uk/decision/DRN-3959411.pdf.

respondent to pay for representatives for the complainant as well.

CHAPTER ELEVEN

DETERMINING THE COMPLAINT: THE FOS'S 'FAIR AND REASONABLE' APPROACH

This chapter focuses on the FOS's approach to resolving complaints.

Given the very wide variety of complaints seen by the FOS, it is not possible to set out all factors that will play a part in the eventual outcome, but the overall approach of the FOS is clear. As set out in FSMA, s. 228(2): '*A complaint is to be determined by reference to what is, in the opinion of the ombudsman, fair and reasonable in all the circumstances of the case.*'[1]

This is supplemented by DISP 3.6.4R:

> '*In considering what is fair and reasonable in all the circumstances of the case, the Ombudsman will take into account: (1) relevant: (a) law and regulations; (b) regulators' rules, guidance and standards; (c) codes of practice; and (2) (where appropriate) what he considers to have been good industry practice at the relevant time.*'

When considering a complaint, and what is fair and reasonable, the FOS is not merely reviewing the respondent's decisions to consider whether it was within a range of reasonable outcomes. Instead, the FOS makes its own assessment of what is fair and reasonable on the facts of the case.[2]

---

1 Repeated in DISP 3.6.1R.

2 *R (Aviva Life and Pensions (UK) Ltd) v FOS* [2017] EWHC 352 (Admin) at [58].

Application of the law

One of the innovations of the FOS is that it is not required to apply English law.[3] Instead, as DISP 3.6.4R states, the ombudsman will take English law into account, along with other relevant rules and standards and good industry practice. It follows that a case can succeed before the FOS which would fail if considered by the court.

It has been suggested that this means that the FOS can act unpredictably and arbitrarily, and so breaches the rule of law. The Court of Appeal rejected that argument in *R (Heather Moor & Edgecomb) v FOS* [2008] EWCA Civ 642, holding that there is sufficient certainty as to outcome. It held that that the FOS should apply the relevant law, regulations, rules etc. save in exceptional circumstances and, even then, the FOS is required to address the relevant law and explain why it is not being applied.[4]

In a 'postscript' in *R (Aviva Life and Pensions (UK) Ltd) v FOS* [2017] EWHC 352 (Admin), Jay J expressed concerns about the ability of the FOS to reach conclusions that would be rejected by a court. Why, he asked, should the FOS be allowed to reject a conclusion that the courts had decided is just? In *Options UK Personal Pensions v FOS* [2024] EWCA Civ 541 at [77] ('*Options UK*'), Asplin LJ in the Court of Appeal noted the 'postscript' but said that a clear explanation of the matters taken into account by the ombudsman provides sufficient safeguards.

As to the need for the FOS to explain why it is not following the law, in any particular case, the burden on the FOS seems to be limited.

In *R (IFG Financial Services Ltd) v FOS* [2005] EWHC 1153 (Admin), the respondent firm had obtained leading counsel's opinion as to the law of causation. The FOS accepted that the opinion was an accurate statement of the law, but it did not apply it. The court upheld the decision, stating that it is sufficient for the FOS ombudsman to set out

3 Confirmed in *R (Heather Moor & Edgecomb) v FOS* [2008] EWCA Civ 642 at [36]. See also *R (Charles Street Securities Europe LLP) v FOS* [2023] EWHC 448 (Admin) at [57].

4 *R (Heather Moor & Edgecomb) v FOS* [2008] EWCA Civ 642 at [49]. Also see *Aviva v FOS* [2017] EWHC 352 (Admin) at [59].

what he considers to be fair and reasonable in the circumstances.[5]

Similarly, in *R (Charles Street Securities Europe LLP) v FOS* [2023] EWHC 448 (Admin), the court upheld the ombudsman's decision on causation, as distinct from the common law principles of causation. It was for the ombudsman to determine what weight to give to certain factors when considering what is fair and reasonable in the circumstances. That the claimant did not agree with the weight accorded to them did not render the decision irrational.[6]

In *Options UK*, Asplin LJ emphasised that the FOS does not need to go through every possible contractual and tortious duty and expressly state why the FOS is going beyond them. On the facts of that case, it was inherent in the ombudsman's reasoning why he was going beyond contractual provisions. That reasoning was sufficient.[7]

On the other hand, if the FOS misconstrues a contract, as a question of law, then that may be sufficient to quash the decision, as in *R (TF Global Markets) v FOS* [2020] EWHC 3178 (Admin). Although not addressed specifically in the judgment, it may be said that the FOS can only take the law into account if it got the law wrong.

As to the ability to challenge FOS decisions, see Chapter 17.

Application of the FCA Rules

When reaching its conclusions, the FOS will accord significant weight to the FCA Rules, including the high level 'Principles'.[8] A breach of the Principles is a sufficient basis to find in favour of the complainant,[9] even

5 See paragraph 90.

6 At [119].

7 At [78]–[79].

8 *R (British Bankers Association) v FSA* [2011] EWHC 999 (Admin) at [75]-[78]; *R (Berkeley Burke) v FOS* [2018] EWHC 2878 (Admin).

9 In *Options UK Personal Pensions v FOS* [2024] EWCA Civ 541 at [85], the Court of Appeal considered that a breach of specific rules was inherent in the finding that the Principles had been breached, but in any event agreed at [93] with the *British*

if the respondent otherwise complied with all of the specific rules in the FCA Handbook.[10] This is despite the fact that the breach of a Principle would not in itself give rise to a cause of action in law.

As above, if the FOS concludes that the respondent has acted unreasonably, despite following all specific FCA Rules on the matter, the FOS should provide sufficient reasons to explain why it does so.[11]

Could the FOS conclude that a firm ought to have acted in a particular way despite such actions being contrary to a specific Rule? In *R (Berkeley Burke) v FOS* [2018] EWHC 2878 (Admin), it was argued that the FOS had done this by requiring a SIPP operator to refuse to trade, despite a Rule requiring the trade to be effected. The court agreed with the FOS that the specific Rule was not breached in that case: the relevant Rule was concerned only with the mechanics of trading, not any decision as to whether to trade or not.[12] In principle, however, it appeared to be accepted that the FOS would have erred in law if it had concluded that the firm ought to have done something that the Rules required it not to do.

Where the FCA has made relevant findings

There may be cases in which the FCA has considered some of the specific issues that are part of the complaint before the FOS. This is particularly likely where the FCA has concluded that there are systemic problems in an area of financial services (such as PPI). There can be no doubt that the FOS is entitled to take those findings into account when reaching its own decisions.

On the other hand, in *R (Critchley) v FOS* [2019] EWHC 3036 (Admin),

---

Bankers Association case that a complaint could be upheld for a breach of the Principles.

10 *R (British Bankers Association) v FSA* [2011] EWHC 999 (Admin) at [184]. See also *R (Berkeley Burke) v FOS* [2018] EWHC 2878 (Admin).

11 *R (British Bankers Association) v FSA* [2011] EWHC 999 (Admin) at [186].

12 See [122]–[132].

the court rejected a judicial review in which it was argued that the FOS was misapplying a presumption of inducement in FCA rules relating to the mis-selling of PPI policies. Having concluded that the FOS had correctly interpreted the rules, the court did not interfere with the FOS's decision.[13]

The FOS will not always dismiss a complaint just because the FCA has looked into the same or similar matter and concluded that there is not a significant problem. This was the position in *R (Full Circle Asset Management Ltd) v FOS* [2017] EWHC 323 (Admin), where the FCA had expressed a view on the riskiness of an investment portfolio. Without disagreeing with that conclusion, the FOS was still entitled to conclude that the portfolio was inappropriate for the requirements of an individual investor.

Use of an ombudsman's own knowledge

DISP 3.6.4R, together with the inquisitorial role of the FOS,[14] means that a decision may be based on the ombudsman's personal knowledge and experience of the financial services industry.[15]

The courts recognise that there is a risk that an ombudsman may use hindsight, particularly when change in an area of the industry has been rapid and unexpected. It has been suggested that the use of personal experience by an ombudsman should depend on the type of question in issue: if the matter is straightforward and uncontroversial, then the ombudsman can proceed based on experience, but there should be greater circumspection if the matter is more complicated.[16]

---

13 See also *R (Berkeley Burke) v FOS* [2018] EWHC 2878 (Admin) at [82]: '*there is an important distinction between (i) construction of the rules (Which is a matter for the court), and (ii) the application of those rules to the facts of the case, which is a matter for the decision-maker.*'

14 See Chapter 7.

15 *R (Williams) v FOS* [2008] EWHC 2142 (Admin) at [26].

16 *R (Williams) v FOS* [2008] EWHC 2142 (Admin) at [45].

That said, even if a FOS decision does rest on the personal experience of complicated matters, it will still be difficult to overturn the decision, given the difficulties in judicially reviewing the FOS: see Chapter 17.

CHAPTER TWELVE

PAYING FOR THE COMPLAINT

Complainants to the FOS are not required to pay anything to bring their complaint. Instead, the FOS is paid for by the financial services industry through levies and case fees.[1]

This book does not consider the intricacies of the levies and the fees, but readers may be interested the overall structure of the fees paid per complaint in a standard case.

Most complaints to the FOS are 'chargeable cases', meaning that the respondent may be required to pay for it, depending on how many complaints have been made about that respondent in the same financial year or whether the respondent can benefit from an exemption.[2] The same fees apply to respondents under the compulsory jurisdiction and voluntary jurisdiction.[3]

Chargeable cases include any complaint, except those where:[4]

1. The FOS decides that the complaint should not proceed because the complainant is not an eligible complainant, because the complaint falls outside the FOS's jurisdiction, or because the complaint should be dismissed without considering its merits (see Chapter 8).

2. At a later stage, the FOS concludes that complaint should be

---

1 As envisaged by FSMA, s. 234.

2 E.g. cash plan health providers and small friendly providers: FEES 5.5B.3R and 5.5B.4G.

3 FEES 5.5B.2G.

4 From the Glossary definition of Chargeable Case within the FCA Handbook.

dismissed as frivolous or vexatious (also see Chapter 8).

3. The complaint has already been dealt with by the respondent under the terms of a consumer redress scheme.

All complaints are chargeable unless they fall within the exceptions above.

At the time of writing, the first three chargeable complaints about a respondent within a financial year are without charge to that respondent. The FOS starts charging most respondents from the fourth chargeable case, at a cost of £650.[5]

Respondents must pay for chargeable cases whether the complaint is successful or not. Whilst some might see this as unfair, the courts have confirmed the validity of the charges.[6]

As outlined in Chapter 7, the FOS has recently consulted on proposals requiring Claims Management Companies ('CMCs') and other professional representatives to pay up to £250 to lodge a case with the FOS. If the case is resolved in favour of the consumer, however, the fee would be reduced to £75. Importantly, the fees are only to apply to CMCs and professional representatives. Consumers who bring cases directly to FOS, as well as friends, family members, charities and voluntary organisations acting on their behalf, would still be able to do so free of charge.[7]

---

5 FEES 5 Annex 3R, Part 1.

6 *R (Heather Moor & Edgecomb) v FOS* [2008] EWCA Civ 643.

7 For further details see: https://www.financial-ombudsman.org.uk/news/charges-professional-representatives-detailed-first-time-new-ombudsman-service-consultation.

CHAPTER THIRTEEN

FOS AWARDS

This chapter outlines the powers which the FOS has to make awards in favour of complainants who have been successful.

As regards the compulsory jurisdiction, the FOS's powers are contained in s.229(2) of FSMA. The determination may include an award against the respondent of such amount as the FOS considers 'fair compensation' for 'loss and damage'. It can also include a direction that the respondent takes 'such steps' in relation to the complainant as the FOS considers just and appropriate.

The effect of these provisions is that the FOS has the power, in relation to the compulsory jurisdiction, to make both monetary awards and to order the taking of other steps. It does not matter whether the court would have the power to make an order in those terms.

DISP 4.2.4R provides that the FOS has the same powers to make determinations and awards under the voluntary jurisdiction as it has under the compulsory jurisdiction. FOS determinations, if accepted by the complainant in time, will be binding on the VJ Participant and can be enforced in court.

The FOS also has powers in relation to the award of costs.

Monetary awards

<u>In respect of what losses can an award be made?</u>

DISP 3.7.2R allows the FOS to award compensation for:

1. Financial loss, which can include consequential loss or prospective loss; or

2. Pain and suffering; or

3. Damage to reputation; or

4. Distress or inconvenience.

The position is slightly different for complaints in respect of consumer redress schemes, under FSMA s.404B. In such cases, the FOS has jurisdiction to make a money award of such amount as the FOS determines the respondent should make or should have made to the complainant.[1] In essence, the FOS operates as an appeal mechanism from the consumer redress scheme, and if the complaint is upheld the FOS will usually make whatever money award the complainant should have been awarded under the redress scheme.

How are monetary awards calculated?

A monetary award can be made in such amount as the FOS considers fair compensation for loss or damage suffered by the complainant. The award can compensate for financial loss or any other loss or damage of a 'specified kind'.[2] Although not explicitly stated, it appears that these 'specified kinds' of losses are those referred to above, set out in DISP 3.7.2R.

The primary aim of a monetary award is to be compensatory. The FOS's website confirms that, if a complaint is upheld, its aim generally will be to put the complainant in the position they would have been in if '*things hadn't gone wrong*'.[3]

But the FOS is not required to apply the same principles as a court would when working out what compensation should be paid. The award must be for what the FOS considers 'fair compensation' (implying some degree of subjectivity), subject to the limits of reasonableness and what can be challenged on a judicial review.

1 DISP 3.7.2AG.

2 FSMA, s.229(2) and (3).

3 See https://www.financial-ombudsman.org.uk/businesses/resolving-complaint/understanding-compensation.

For more information on challenges by judicial review, see Chapter 17. As explained in that chapter, such challenges are rarely successful. So, in *R (IFG Financial Services Ltd) v FOS* [2005] EWHC 1153 (Admin) ('*IFG*'), the court rejected a challenge to a FOS decision where the FOS had essentially refused to apply orthodox principles about remoteness of damages[4] and scope of liability[5] when assessing the complainants' damages. The FOS had referred to the relevant principles when coming to its determination, but simply decided that it was not fair and reasonable to apply them. The mere fact this result differed from that which would follow from a strict application of English law was not enough to result in a successful challenge.

In terms of the reasons that the FOS needed to give when reaching its conclusions as to how damages should be calculated, all that was required on the facts of *IFG* was that the FOS made clear what it thought to be fair and reasonable in the circumstances.[6]

Compensation for pecuniary losses

Often the FOS may ask a respondent to compensate a complainant for an investment loss or for being deprived of the use of their money. The former will be awarded where, for instance, the complainant is found to have purchased an unsuitable product. Where that is so, the FOS will normally award compensation based on what would have happened to the complainant's money if the investment had not been made.

The FOS recognises that compensation should depend upon where the complainant would have put their money. A customer who did not want to risk their capital is likely to be awarded risk-free investments (calculated as the average rate for one-year fixed-rate bonds as published by the Bank of England).

On the other hand, there may be a specific alternative investment that

---

4 i.e. the notion that, to be recoverable, a loss must be reasonably foreseeable.

5 See *South Australia Asset Management Corp v York Montague Ltd* [1997] AC 191.

6 At [90].

was discussed at the time of the original advice. In that case, the FOS may conclude that one of those alternatives provides the benchmark.

However, in practice, it is often impossible to know precisely what the complainant would have done with their money. To address these situations, the FOS will usually order the respondent to pay compensation by reference to a relevant benchmark: e.g., the FTSE UK Private Investors Income Total Return Index.[7] Alternatively, perhaps, compensation might be calculated on the basis 50% would have been left in a bank, with 50% invested into the benchmark fund.

The FOS's guidance makes clear that the amount of risk the complainant would have taken on is important and will have a bearing on the benchmark measures that may be used.[8]

The FOS will then normally tell the business to work out the difference between the complainant's financial position in respect of the mis-sold investment and the relevant benchmark.

The respondent may also be ordered to repay the fees it charged for advice if, as part of the steps which the complainant needs to take to put matters right, they will have to pay further fees.

Simple interest will be added to this at a rate of 8%. But no such refund will be given where the respondent has already taken action to correct a situation without charging a further fee.[9]

Where the complainant no longer has the investment product at the date their award is assessed, the FOS will normally require the respondent to pay: (i) compensation to cover the investment loss from the date the investment was taken out to the date it was disposed of; and (ii) interest from the date of disposal until the date of payment (normally at a rate of

---

7 See https://www.financial-ombudsman.org.uk/businesses/resolving-complaint/understanding-compensation/compensation-investment-complaints. For an example of this, see *R (Linear Investments Ltd) v FOS* [2024] EWHC 1428 (Admin) at [58].

8 Ibid.

9 Ibid. under the heading '*Advice fees and commission*'.

8% simple).[10]

Often, complainants will still hold the investment at the time their award is made. Provided the investment is liquid and its value ascertainable, the value of the continued investment will be taken into account. The complainant may also then keep their investment. Should the complainant then suffer further losses on the investment after a FOS award, they will not normally be entitled to seek redress for these losses from the FOS.

However, where the market is illiquid the complainant will not be able to sell the investment and FOS will have the difficulty that it cannot be sure about what value, if any, the consumer might be able to realise from the investment. In this case, the FOS will normally require the investment to be transferred to the business and the complainant will be awarded the full value of their losses.[11]

This result, however, can be complicated by the FOS's compensatory cap (see below). If the FOS makes a recommendation above the cap, and the respondent does not follow it, then the complainant will be able to keep their investment in addition to the money award. [12]

As an alternative, the FOS may always award compensation on the basis that the investment should be treated as if it were rescinded. This approach usually arises where the complainant has entered into a contract with the respondent which has produced no value for the customer. A typical example might be a PPI policy which has now expired. This will normally involve the respondent repaying the complainant premiums that were charged, plus simple interest at 8%.[13]

---

10 Ibid. under the heading '*The consumer no longer has the investment*'.

11 Ibid. under the heading '*The investment is 'illiquid' or suspended.*

12 At least, this was the FOS's former position, as set out in its (now deleted) technical notes: https://web.archive.org/web/20180812010634/http://www.financial-ombudsman.org.uk/publications/technical_notes/calculating-comp-investment-complaint.html#3b.

13 https://www.financial-ombudsman.org.uk/businesses/resolving-complaint/under

Contributory fault

Although not mentioned in DISP, nor the FOS's website, FOS awards can in principle be reduced for contributory negligence. In one FOS decision, the principle was described as follows:

> '*Contributory negligence is an important consideration when making an award. The concept derives from law and can be explained as weighing up whether a consumer should have done something to mitigate their losses, or if they should share some responsibility because they were partly to blame.*'[14]

This issue often arises in relation to payment and other scams. The FOS regularly holds firms liable for losses sustained by their customers through such scams, but will also consider whether the consumer should bear some of the losses.

On the other hand, in *R (Linear Investments Ltd) v FOS* [2024] EWHC 1428 (Admin), the FOS decided not to reduce an award by reference to the complainant's inaccurate answers to his client classification. The FOS concluded that the firm incorrectly classified the complainant and, but for that fault, he would have suffered no losses. This conclusion was upheld by the court.

Compensation for non-pecuniary losses

DISP 3.7.2R allows the FOS to make money awards in respect of certain non-pecuniary losses for pain and suffering, damage to reputation, and distress or inconvenience. The FOS collectively refers to these as awards for 'trouble and upset'.

Such awards may be made if the ombudsman considers the complainant faced obstacles or difficulties that could have been avoided if the firm had

---

standing-compensation/compensation-investment-complaints under the heading '*Rescinded investments*'.

[14] Decision Reference DRN-3840917.

handled things differently.[15] Usually these awards will be made therefore when the FOS makes a finding that the complainant has received poor service but cannot identify any real loss. Examples provided by the FOS for when such an award will be made include: (i) when a customer had to contact a firm repeatedly to get something '*quite basic sorted out*' such as updating their address; or (ii) where a firm underpays a customer's pension for a significant amount of time, meaning they experienced reduced living standards that are likely to have caused considerable long-term distress.[16]

Nonetheless, a '*certain level of frustration and minor annoyance is expected*' so, for an award to be made, the FOS needs to see '*the impact of a mistake was more than someone would expect to experience as part of everyday life*'.[17] In this respect, minor delays due to a business's phone line being busy will not attract an award.

Such awards will not be made where the obstacle or difficulty faced by the customer was outside of the firm's control or caused by a third party.

When determining whether such an award will be made, the FOS will consider all the circumstances of the complaint. It will also consider:

1. Whether the customer is vulnerable and if this could be more severely impacted by a mistake. In these circumstances, a higher award may be granted to reflect this, and particularly where the firm was aware of the customer's vulnerability.

2. If the award relates to lost time, the FOS may ask for evidence of how much time the customer has spent on the issue. The FOS would consider, for example, any lost wages. However, in such circumstances the award will not be calculated on the basis of an hourly rate. The FOS '*don't make awards based on units of time,*

15 See https://www.financial-ombudsman.org.uk/businesses/resolving-complaint/understanding-compensation/compensation-for-distress-or-inconvenience.

16 Ibid.

17 See https://www.financial-ombudsman.org.uk/businesses/resolving-complaint/understanding-compensation/compensation-for-distress-or-inconvenience.

and everyone's time is precious regardless of what a customer earns. Instead we decide fair compensation by looking at the overall impact the business's mistake had on the customer'.[18]

3. Whether the customer could have taken steps to reduce the impact of the mistake on them. The FOS will carefully consider the circumstances to decide what impact directly flows from the original error.

Experience suggests that FOS awards are typically in the region of a couple of hundred pounds at most, or the FOS may just order the respondent to provide a simple apology.

Nonetheless, the FOS provides the following guidance as to what level of award may be made:

- Apologies or awards for less than £100 are used to compensate a one-off incident or occurrence, such as a small administrative error or a short delay.

- An award between £100 and up to £300 might be suitable where there have been repeated small errors, or a larger single mistake, requiring a reasonable amount of effort to resolve. The FOS suggest that these typically result in disruption that lasts a few days or even weeks.

- An award of over £300 and up to around £750 may be made where the impact of a mistake has caused considerable distress, upset and worry – and/or significant inconvenience and disruption that takes considerable time to resolve. Typically, this lasts over many weeks or months, but it could also be a mistake that has had a serious short-term impact.

- Awards of over £750 and up to around £1,500 are reserved for instances where a firm's mistake has caused substantial distress, upset and worry – '*even potentially a serious offence or*

[18] Ibid.

humiliation'.[19]

- Awards of over £1,500 and up to around £5,000 are appropriate where the mistakes caused sustained distress, potentially affecting someone's health, or severe disruption to daily life typically lasting more than one year.

- Finally, awards can be made for over £5,000 but these are reserved for the '*most extreme impact we see*'.[20]

What form does a monetary award take?

There are two alternatives here.

First, the FOS can simply state, as a figure, the amount which it thinks the respondent should pay. For most complaints, and particularly those concerning distress, damage to reputation and other non-pecuniary losses, this is likely to be the form which the award takes.

The second possibility is that the FOS specifies a formula by which compensation can be calculated. This is more often used in circumstances where compensation for a mis-sold investment is granted. In these types of case, it will be the duty of the respondent to carry out the relevant calculation. The FOS will not normally check the calculations provided by the respondent.[21]

---

19 https://www.financial-ombudsman.org.uk/businesses/resolving-complaint/understanding-compensation/compensation-for-distress-or-inconvenience.

20 Ibid.

21 https://www.financial-ombudsman.org.uk/businesses/resolving-complaint/understanding-compensation/compensation-investment-complaints under the heading '*Handling compensation – what you need to do*'.

How much can a monetary award be for?

The monetary awards that the FOS can make are limited by its rules. These have increased over the years, leading to a current maximum award of £430,000. This is a significant increase on the maximum award of £100,000, which applied until 1 January 2012.

The current maximums depend on a combination of the date of the act or omission complained about, and the date that the complaint was referred to the FOS. A table under DISP 3.7.4R sets out the maximums, and is updated on 1 April each year to uprate the maximums by reference to CPI inflation:

Date complaint referred	**Date of act or omission**	
	Before 1 April 2019	On or after 1 April 2019
Before 1 January 2012	£100,000	n/a
Before 1 April 2019 but on or after 1 January 2012	£150,000	n/a
On or after 1 April 2019	£160,000	£350,000
On or after 1 April 2020	£160,000	£355,000
On or after 1 April 2022	£170,000	£375,000
On or after 1 April 2023	£190,000	£415,000
On or after 1 April 2024	£195,000	£430,000

Accordingly, a complaint relating to events in 2010, but referred on 2 April 2024, can lead to compensation of up to £195,000. A complaint relating to events in 2020, referred on 2 April 2024, can lead to compensation of up to £430,000.

Section 404B(5) of FSMA provides that awards in respect of complaints arising out of consumer redress schemes are subject to the same limits.

When judging whether an award exceeds this limit, the FOS is to exclude the interest on the award, any costs awarded, and any interest on costs.[22] Once these further awards are taken into account, the overall award can therefore exceed £430,000.

Some serious financial mis-selling claims will seek losses far in excess of the FOS's statutory limit. At least where a complainant is represented by lawyers, it is questionable whether such a complaint should be submitted to the FOS at all, absent peculiar features. Indeed, at least historically, the FOS would itself write to complainants where this is the case so that they could decide whether to continue using the FOS procedures and take legal advice.[23] This is necessary in view of the fact that, as we shall we see, accepting a FOS award will normally preclude a claim in court for the sums in excess of the maximum that the FOS can award.[24]

The FOS might also dismiss complaints as being unsuitable for its procedures (see Chapter 8).[25]

Nevertheless, where the FOS considers that fair compensation would require a payment in excess of its maximum, it may require payment of the maximum and recommend that the respondent pay a larger sum.[26] It

22 DISP 3.7.5G.

23 https://web.archive.org/web/20180506225427/http://www.financial-ombudsman.org.uk/publications/technical_notes/compensation.html#maximumlimit.

24 See also https://www.financial-ombudsman.org.uk/consumers/expect/compensation where the FOS notes: '*If you accept an award made in an ombudsman's final decision, it's unlikely you'll be able to take the business to court for more compensation later. We can't give you legal advice about this, so you'll need to speak to get independent legal advice if that's something you're considering, before you accept any award.*'

25 DISP 3.3.4AR (5) and 3.3.4BG (1). For recent statistics on complaints dismissed on these bases see: https://www.financial-ombudsman.org.uk/files/324276/ADR-annual-activity-report-2022-2023.pdf.

26 FSMA, s.229 (5) and DISP 3.7.6G. This power applies to the voluntary jurisdiction as well.

will be for the respondent to decide whether to follow this recommendation and, to the extent that the award exceeds the FOS maximum award, it cannot be enforced in the courts.

Given the limits on monetary awards, complainants may submit multiple complaints about very similar issues. An investor who complains that she was advised to invest in Investment X, Investment Y and Investment Z, all of which were unsuitable, may therefore submit three complaints. The rules allow the FOS to consider complaints relating to 'connected circumstances' together and make a monetary award in respect of each complaint.[27]

It follows that a complainant can be awarded multiples of the maximum monetary award in appropriate circumstances. There is little guidance on when it is appropriate to 'split' complaints in this way, but anecdotally it has been suggested that the FOS actively encourages this approach.

Interest award

The FOS has the power to order the payment of interest, at a rate and from a date set by the FOS. [28]

For complaints in respect of consumer redress schemes, the FOS has the power to order that interest is payable on any amount which is not paid by the date specified in the award for payment.[29]

The FOS's usual practice is to award interest at 'the statutory rate', currently 8% simple interest.[30] Implicitly, this is a reference to the Judgments Act 1838. It is not clear why the FOS uses this yardstick. The 1838 Act applies to interest payable on judgments, and the courts do not

---

27 DISP 3.5.3G.

28 DISP 3.7.1R (2) and DISP 3.7.8R.

29 DISP 3.7.8AG.

30 https://www.financial-ombudsman.org.uk/businesses/resolving-complaint/understanding-compensation/compensation-investment-complaints under the heading '*Interest where the customer is 'deprived of money*'.

generally apply it for periods prior to judgment. The use of the 8% rate by the FOS means that FOS interest awards are usually in excess of those that the complainant could expect to be awarded in court.

Interest will continue to run until the date of payment.

The FOS should be astute to ensure that an award of interest does not overlap with the relief given in their main monetary award. For many financial mis-selling claims, this will mean that an award of 8% interest is not appropriate, because the award will take into account the value of the investments that the complainant should have at the date of the award. Interest in these circumstances would amount to double recovery.

Costs awards

The FOS has the power to make awards in respect of the complainant's costs.[31]

Whilst many of the complainants before the FOS will not have representation or professional advisers assisting them, and such awards are unlikely to be common,[32] the FOS may make an award in such amount as it considers to be fair, to cover some or all of the costs that were reasonably incurred by the complainant. Interest may also be ordered to be paid on costs.[33]

Three points are worth noting about these powers. The first is that, as stated, they will not be common or usual.[34] If the case is sufficiently large or complex to justify representation of some description, there may be an argument about whether litigation would have been a more appropriate

---

31 DISP 3.7.1R(3). This power is derived from FSMA, s. 230. By s.230(7), a costs award is enforceable in the same way as other awards for money in accordance with FSMA, Schedule 17, Part II, paragraph 16: see Chapter 15.

32 DISP 3.7.10G.

33 DISP 3.7.9R.

34 See also https://www.financial-ombudsman.org.uk/businesses/resolving-complaint/understanding-compensation: '*Costs awards aren't common, but we need to think about what's fair in each individual case*'.

avenue for the dispute. In practice, we are not aware of any complaints where costs have been awarded.[35]

Secondly, the FOS only has the power to make awards in respect of a complainant's costs. Respondents are not able to recover their costs. This is specifically prohibited by s.230(3) of FSMA. Attempts by a firm to recover costs by complaining about the FOS are also unlikely to be successful (as to which, see Chapter 19).

Thirdly, the costs award can only be in respect of those that were reasonably incurred. This will require an assessment by the FOS. Presumably, similar factors as to those which a court takes into account when assessing costs will be considered – including, the amount at stake, the complexity of the arguments, the level of fees, and the conduct of the parties (and any offers of reparation that may have been made).

Directions

In addition to its powers to make monetary awards, the FOS can order that a respondent take steps in relation to the complainant which the FOS considers 'just and appropriate'.[36] This is obviously inspired by the court's power to grant injunctions and specific performance. But the rules confirm that the FOS's power to issue directions can be made whether or not a court could order those steps to be taken.[37]

The usual factors that are considered by courts when assessing whether to grant injunctions or specific performance will doubtless be relevant

---

[35] See, for example, https://www.financial-ombudsman.org.uk/decision/DRN-4312583.pdf where the FOS concluded that it would have been difficult for the complainant to progress a complaint without legal support, but still declined to make any award of costs.

[36] DISP 3.7.11R. Unless the complaint is a 'relevant complaint' within the meaning of s. 404B(3) of FSMA. In these circumstances, a direction may require the respondent to take such action as the ombudsman determines the respondent should take (or should have taken) under the scheme: DISP 3.7.11AG.

[37] FSMA, s. 229(2)(b); DISP 3.7.11R.

when the FOS assesses what is just and appropriate.

A direction may be enforceable by a court by way of an injunction (see Chapter 15).[38]

However, a direction will not be enforced to the extent that it imposes a cost on the respondent in excess of the cap that would apply to monetary awards.[39] Whether an award is a direction or a monetary award will depend on its substance, not its form. So, a determination that requires the payment of money to the complainant or for his benefit is a money award.[40]

Where a direction is made which would cost the respondent more than the FOS maximum award to comply with, it will be subject to an implied limitation that compliance is only required up to the cap.[41] One can imagine scenarios where the application of this rule will be very difficult. If an insurance company is directed to make good defects caused by subsidence covered by an insurance policy, for example, it may be unknowable how much the remedial works will cost: would the court issue an injunction requiring the insurance company to start on the works, on the basis that they can stop once their costs hit the FOS maximum award? Such issues have not, as far as we are aware, arisen in practice.

<u>Publication of awards</u>

Since 1 April 2013, the FOS has reported most of its determinations on its website. It reports all of its decisions, unless it is of the view that publication is inappropriate.[42] These reports are anonymised in respect

---

38 See s.229(9) of FSMA.

39 *Bunney v Burns Anderson PLC* [2007] EWHC 1240 (Ch).

40 Ibid at [68].

41 *R (Aviva Life and Pensions (UK) Ltd) v FOS* [2017] EWHC 352 at [54].

42 DISP 3.6.8G (1).

of the complainant,[43] but bear the name of the respondent against whom the complaint was referred.

The FOS also publishes data about the number of complaints against individual firms, and the number of complaints that are upheld against such firms.[44]

---

43 DISP 3.6.8G (2), unless the complainant consents.

44 Seethe FOS's 'Half-yearly complaints data' showing the number of complaints against financial businesses. The data for H1 2024 is available at: https://www.financial-ombudsman.org.uk/data-insight/half-yearly-complaints-data/half-yearly-complaints-data-h1-2024.

CHAPTER FOURTEEN

HOW AN AWARD IS ACCEPTED OR REJECTED, AND THE CONSEQUENCES

This chapter is concerned with the position following an ombudsman's final decision.

The final decision requires the complainant to notify the FOS before a specified date accepting or rejecting the determination. The FOS is required to notify the respondent of the outcome.[1]

This gives rise to three possibilities. The first, and simplest, is that the complainant rejects the determination. The FOS award will then be of no effect, and the complainant will generally be free to pursue whatever other remedies they wish. The only possible complication is the extent to which a Court would be entitled to have reference to the FOS decision within subsequent litigation (discussed in Chapter 16 below).

The second possibility is that the complainant fails to notify the FOS whether they accept or reject the determination. If this happens, under the compulsory jurisdiction the complainant is deemed to have rejected the award[2] unless the complainant later seeks to accept the determination and the FOS considers that the failure to reply was caused by 'exceptional circumstances'.[3] Although there is no explicit guidance on this rule, this will raise similar issues as those which arise when the FOS is considering whether there were exceptional circumstances which justify a departure

---

1 FSMA, s.228. DISP 4.2.4R states that the FOS has the same powers to make determinations and awards under the voluntary jurisdiction as they have under the compulsory jurisdiction.

2 FSMA, s.228(6).

3 DISP 3.6.6R(4A).

from the time limits to bringing a complaint (see Chapter 6).

Slightly different rules apply to the voluntary jurisdiction. DISP 4.2.5R states that, provided the complainant accepts an award within the time specified for doing so, the determination will be binding on the VJ Participant. That means that, if the award is not accepted in time, it will not be binding.

The third possibility is that the determination is accepted by the complainant. Where this happens, the determination is binding on both the complainant and the respondent and is stated to be 'final'.[4] For the voluntary jurisdiction, a determination is simply said to be 'binding' on the VJ Participant, and enforceable in court, with no suggestion that it is binding on the complainant.[5]

The effect of acceptance

Once a FOS determination is accepted, the complaint is resolved once and for all. This will preclude a complainant from accepting an award for, say, £150,000, but then trying to commence court proceedings for any losses in excess of this.

That was the position in *Clark v In Focus Asset Management & Tax Solutions Ltd* [2014] EWCA Civ 118 ('*Clark*').[6] The claimant accepted an award under the compulsory jurisdiction but stated that this acceptance was without prejudice to their right to bring further court proceedings. The claimant commenced proceedings for the rest of their alleged losses.

The Court of Appeal ruled that the award was binding and precluded legal proceedings in which the cause of action was constituted by the same facts as those on which the complaint was based. This is because

4 FSMA, s.228(5).

5 DISP 4.2.5R.

6 See also *Andrews v SBJ Benefit Consultants Ltd* [2010] EWHC 2875 (Ch), which is to similar effect.

FOS decisions are sufficiently judicial to engage the principle of *res judicata*. The court rejected the idea that, because the FOS's jurisdiction is there to aid consumers, it should be seen as additional to their right to also bring complaints before a court, even after a FOS determination had been accepted by them. Nor was it determinative that the FOS dealt with complaints rather than causes of action. For *res judicata* to occur, it was enough that the FOS decides a question posed by facts constituting a cause of action.

Arden LJ said at paragraph [77]:

> '*it is sufficient that he decides whether the facts underlying a cause of action give rise to any claim as between the complainant and the adviser and whether the claimant has any remedy against the adviser relative to those facts. The fact that the remedy is not the same as would be awarded in a court of law is also not a requirement of* res judicata*...if the complainant were (unwisely) to accept an award offering him only an apology,* res judicata *would apply if he chose to bring court proceedings. His wiser course would be to reject the award altogether in those circumstances.*'

Arden LJ also gave guidance on how the court, when faced with a further action which had arguably already been determined by the FOS, should approach whether the second action was permissible. She said, at paragraph [79] that:

> '*...the court would have to consider whether this was the same complaint and if so whether the ombudsman had determined the question raised by this complaint. The court would have to look at the detailed documentation.*'

In the Northern Irish decision of *Morton v First Trust Financial Services Ltd* [2015] NIQB 46, Weatherup J declined to strike out a claim on the basis that a later court action was an abuse of process. He said that it would have required more than an analysis on the papers.

Accordingly, not all later court actions will be barred by the doctrine of *res judicata*, even if a determination was accepted. This will depend on the whether '*the substance of the proceedings asserted before the courts are the same as that before the Ombudsman Service*'.[7] It is, however, clear that an attempt to bring a court claim to get around the monetary limits on FOS awards is impermissible.

The burden of showing that the facts constituting the cause of action relied on in the later court proceedings formed the basis of the FOS complaint is on the defendant.[8]

Clark was a case that concerned *res judicata* - i.e. whether the cause of action had already been decided on. The courts have long recognised that even though a claim may not strictly be subject to *res judicata*, it may nevertheless be an abuse of process because it is one which could and should have been brought in earlier proceedings. This is so-called *Henderson v Henderson* abuse.[9] Whilst the Court of Appeal did not find it necessary to consider whether the *Henderson* rule would have applied on the facts of *Clark*, once it is recognised a FOS award may give rise to *res judicata* this ought to mean that the *Henderson* doctrine can also apply. The Northern Irish Courts have reached the same conclusion (see the decision of Weatherup J in *Morton*, above).

It remains to be seen whether the same logic applies to the doctrine of issue estoppel. For example, if an accepted FOS decision held that a particular representation was made by either party, would that finding bind the parties in subsequent litigation under a different cause of action? The *res judicata* logic, above, might suggest that issue estoppels can also arise, but it would be surprising if the court were bound by a decision reached by a non-judicial body such as the FOS.

---

7 *Clark v In Focus Asset Management & Tax Solutions Ltd* [2014] EWCA Civ 118 at [89].

8 *Clark v In Focus Focus Asset Management & Tax Solutions Ltd* [2014] EWCA Civ 118 at [81].

9 After *Henderson v Henderson* (1843) 3 Hare 100. The modern law on this rule is set out in *Johnson v Gore Wood & Co* [2000] UKHL 65.

Second actions before the FOS

As to the situation where the complainant brings a complaint before the FOS in respect of the same subject matter as a previous complaint, or the same subject matter as previous litigation, see Chapter 8.

CHAPTER FIFTEEN

ENFORCEMENT OF FOS AWARDS IN COURT

In Chapter 14 we looked at the circumstances under which a court will hear a claim that has already been determined by the FOS, where the FOS's award has been accepted by the complainant. In general, the court will not allow the same complaint to be litigated again in court.

This chapter considers a different situation: where the complainant has accepted a FOS decision and seeks to enforce that award against the respondent.

Enforcement of a FOS award

Once the FOS has determined a complaint and this has been accepted, most respondents will comply and, if needs be, pay any sum found to be due. DISP 3.7.12R obliges respondents to comply promptly with awards, directions, or settlements.

If this does not happen, FSMA contains a mechanism by which the FOS award can be enforced as if it were a court judgment.[1]

By DISP 3.7.7R, the FOS will maintain a register of its awards. A monetary award, including interest, which has been so registered can be enforced as if it were an order of the County Court, should the County Court so order.[2] This means that permission must first be sought from the court before enforcement can be sought. One way of doing that would be to issue a Part 8 Claim Form for such an order.

1 FSMA, s. 229(8) and Sch 17, para 16. DISP 4.2.5R provides that a binding award under the voluntary jurisdiction can be enforced in court by the complainant.

2 FSMA, Sch 17, para 16.

Likewise, an order for directions can be enforced by way of an injunction.[3] In most cases, that can also be done through commencing proceedings using a Part 8 Claim Form.

As set out in Chapter 13, when granting directions, the FOS is not limited to what a court could order.[4] But, as pointed out by Lewison J in *Bunney v Burns Anderson PLC*,[5] this gives rise to a conundrum. If the court could not grant an injunction to take the steps directed (for instance, an apology), then how can it do so under FSMA? Lewison J did not have to answer this question in *Bunney*.

One possibility is that FSMA grants the court the power to make an injunction when it would not otherwise be able to. In equity, there would be no power for a court to order an injunction for, say, an apology; but FSMA may be said to enable it to do so, if contained in a FOS direction.

Nevertheless, injunctions are discretionary. The consequences of a failure to comply with an injunction can be severe (namely, contempt of court). It may be that a judge would refuse to enforce a FOS award that was vague, impossible for the court to supervise, or where exposing the respondent to the possibility of contempt proceedings for non-compliance would be disproportionate.

Set-off against FOS awards

In view of DISP 3.7.12R, and the obligation on respondents to comply with FOS awards promptly, there is a question mark as to how far a respondent can reduce or extinguish the amount of the FOS award where it is owed sums by the complainant (i.e. whether the respondent can exercise a right of set-off against a FOS award).

Where a monetary award is made in favour of a complainant, there seems to be no logical reason why the respondent could not set-off the amount

---

3 FSMA, s. 229(9).

4 DISP 3.7.11R.

5 [2007] EWHC 1240 (Ch) at [74].

of its liability. After all, the financial result to the complainant would be the same. Moreover, the obligation to comply promptly with a FOS award does not say in terms that a set-off is impermissible. This is especially so given that if the FOS award can be enforced as if they were a court judgment, and there are well-established rights of set-off against court judgments.

Limitation Periods

We are not aware of any cases that have tested the limitation period for enforcing a FOS award. It seems likely that the complainant would have six years to enforce their award, either under:

1. Section 24 of the Limitation Act 1980, the time limit for enforcing judgments. This would be on the basis that, providing the court so orders, FOS awards are enforceable as if they were County Court judgments.

2. Section 9 of the Limitation Act 1980, the time limit for actions to recover sums recoverable by statute.

It would then be arguable whether the starting point for limitation purposes is the date of the final decision, or the date that the complainant accepts the award.

CHAPTER SIXTEEN

INTERACTION BETWEEN THE FOS AND LITIGATION

In this chapter, we consider the ways in which FOS complaints interact with litigation in the courts, aside from the questions of *res judicata* and enforcement considered in Chapters 14 and 15.

Stay of proceedings where there is an extant FOS complaint

Normally, a complainant will refer their complaint to the FOS instead of litigation, or with litigation as a fall-back position if the FOS does not find in their favour.

However, it may be that a complainant has no choice but to commence court proceedings due to the imminent expiration of a limitation period,[1] but then wishes to commence proceedings before the FOS. Likewise, the FOS decision may be taking so long that the complainant is forced to issue court proceedings because of limitation concerns.

Nonetheless, the FOS may dismiss a complaint without consideration of the merits where court proceedings are under way, unless all the parties or the court has agreed to stay those proceeding so that the matter may be considered by the FOS.[2]

Accordingly, the two processes should not run concurrently: either the court proceedings are stayed to allow the FOS to consider the complaint, or the proceedings are not stayed, and the FOS rejects the complaint.

In *Templars Estates Ltd v National Westminster Bank PLC* [2016] EWHC

1 Commencing FOS proceedings will not stop limitation from running: *Clarke v Argyle Consulting Ltd* 2011 SLT 180.

2 DISP 3.3.4A R and 3.3.4B G. See Chapter 8.

2020 (Comm), the claimant issued proceedings to avoid the expiration of limitation, but then wished to pursue a FOS complaint. The defendants submitted that the claimants were trying to have their cake and eat it: even if they won before the FOS, there was no guarantee that they would accept the offer and bring an end to the proceedings. The claimant undertook that they would accept any award made by the FOS, and not come back to court if they won before the FOS. On that basis a stay was granted.

Referral by the FOS to another complaints scheme or the court

DISP 3.4 provides the basis upon which the FOS may refer complaints to other complaint schemes or the court. For other complaint schemes, the FOS may so refer where it considers the other scheme to be more suitable, and the complainant consents to the referral.[3]

The FOS has a power, with the complainant's consent, to refer a complaint to court to consider it as a test case. This is set out in DISP 3.4.2R. In summary:

1. Before the FOS has made any determination, the respondent may request a referral, on the basis that the complaint raises '*an important or novel point of law with significant consequences*'.[4] This is quite narrow in scope. It is likely to cover situations where there is a market wide issue.

2. The respondent must provide an undertaking in favour of the complainant that if the complainant or the respondent commences court proceedings in any UK court within six months of the FOS dismissing the claim, the respondent will pay the complainant's reasonable costs of the proceedings.[5]

3. Finally, the FOS must conclude that the complaint raises an

[3] DISP 3.4.1R.

[4] DISP 3.4.2R (1)(a).

[5] DISP 3.4.2R (1)(b).

important or novel point of law with important consequences, which is more suitable for determination by the court as a test case.[6] Factors that the FOS will take into account when making that decision include whether the point of law is central to the dispute, how important it is, the significance to the respondent, the amount at stake, and the remedies that a court could impose.[7]

The admissibility of FOS awards in court proceedings

A party may wish to rely on a particular finding made by the FOS in subsequent litigation. For example, a complainant may have alleged that it received poor advice, but the FOS decides in favour of the financial advisor. If the complainant then pursues the advisor in court, is the advisor entitled to show to the court evidence that the FOS found the advice to be reasonable?

It is a rule of evidence in English courts that a decision in one set of court proceedings is not admissible in later court proceedings to prove the facts that were found by judge in the first set of proceedings. Instead, the same facts must be proven again before the second judge.[8] This is the so-called rule in *Hollington v Hewthorn*. The rule has been criticised and is kept within narrow bounds. For instance, it was not applied where there was a report by the Department of Transport's Air Accident Investigation Branch about an aeroplane accident: the report was admitted in a later civil claim about that accident and was not barred from admission by the *Hollington* rule. The report was from a body with particular expertise, which the court did not itself have, and therefore could be taken into account.[9]

There may be a debate about whether FOS awards are admissible or not in subsequent proceedings as evidence of the facts or conclusions

---

6 DISP 3.4.2R (2).

7 DISP 3.4.3G.

8 *Hollington v F Hewthorn* [1943] KB 587.

9 *Rogers v Hoyle* [2015] QB 265, containing the first instance and appellate decisions.

contained within them. On the one hand, the logic of the courts' deference to the FOS is in part down to its expertise in financial services. On the other hand, the FOS is a tribunal for at least some purposes,[10] and reaches conclusions based on the evidence before it, which would suggest that its findings should not be admissible.

In somewhat similar circumstances, the findings of the FCA have been held to be inadmissible, falling under the rule in *Hollington v Hewthorn.*[11] As far as we are aware, there has been no judicial determination of this question in relation to FOS decisions.

10 *R (Calland) v FOS* [2013] EWHC 1327 (Admin) at [35].

11 *AXA France v Santander Cards* [2022] EWHC 1776 (Comm) at [87].

CHAPTER SEVENTEEN

CHALLENGING FOS DECISIONS IN THE COURTS: JUDICIAL REVIEW AND OTHER OPTIONS

A party that dislikes a final decision from a FOS ombudsman has limited options. There is no appeal process within the FOS rules, and if the complainant accepts the award it becomes final and binding on the respondent.[1] The respondent is obliged to comply with a final decision that the complainant has accepted.[2] A persistent failure to comply with a FOS award may lead to regulatory action by the FCA,[3] potentially even leading to a loss of authorisation.[4]

This chapter sets out the options that exist to challenge FOS awards:

1. The usual method of challenging a FOS award is to seek a judicial review of the decision. This chapter sets out the bases on which judicial review has been sought, and the areas where a review is most likely to be successful.

2. Occasionally, a respondent might seek to challenge an award by waiting for the complainant's claim to enforce the award. In some circumstances, the respondent might be able to defeat the claim by pointing to defects in the FOS award itself, such as an absence of jurisdiction.

---

1 FSMA, s. 228(5). See further Chapter 14.

2 DISP 3.7.12R.

3 For example, see the First Supervisory Notice issued to Alexander David Securities Limited dated 29 April 2022.

4 For example, see the Final Notices issued to Glyn Goodyear dated 14 April 2016; Foreman Financial Services Limited dated 23 October 2017; and Ron Treherne IFA Limited dated 20 May 2021.

In general, the courts have been resistant to challenges to FOS awards. Many firms have tried, and few have succeeded.

The reasons for this are contained within FSMA itself. The FOS was expressly set up to resolve disputes quickly and with minimum formality, based on what the FOS views as fair and reasonable.[5] The courts warn against '*over-active judicial intervention*' and are '*very wary*' of overturning FOS decisions on the facts.[6] That said, the courts have demonstrated more willingness to intervene where it considers the FOS to have overreached its jurisdiction.[7]

Unhappy complainants have also gone to court to argue that the FOS was wrong. Again, it is very difficult to succeed. Most judicial review claims against the FOS fail, though we set out a few examples of successful claims below.

Moreover, the possibility of judicial review proceedings does temper the FOS's approach to complaints. The FOS has been known to reopen complaints (even those it had insisted were closed) in the face of a threat of judicial review proceedings.[8]

Procedure

This is not a book on judicial review procedure, and anybody that is considering such action should consult specialist texts. Nevertheless, there are some basic elements of procedure which any challenging party should be aware of.

Of particular importance in judicial review claims is CPR 54.5(1): '*The claim form must be filed—(a) promptly; and (b) in any event not later than*

5 FSMA, s. 225(1), s. 228(2) and s. 229(2).

6 *R (Norwich and Peterborough Building Society) v FOS* [2002] EWHC 2379 (Admin) at [77]–[78].

7 *R (Bluefin Insurance Services Ltd) v FOS* [2014] EWHC 3413 (Admin).

8 We have personal experience of this. See also the FOS's rejected offer to reconsider its position in *R (Moniak) v FOS* [2023] EWHC 333 (Admin).

3 months after the grounds to make the claim first arose.'

Both elements of the rule are important: judicial review claims have been refused even though they were issued within 3 months of the relevant decision because the court concluded that they were not prompt.

In addition, the applicant is expected to comply with the pre-action protocol for judicial review by sending a letter before claim and giving the defendant 14 days to respond. It is important to note that complying with the pre-action protocol will not extend time for filing the claim form, though it is relevant to the promptness of the claim.

In any case challenging a FOS award, the defendant will be the FOS itself. It will also be appropriate to name the other party to the FOS award as an 'interested party'.[9] So, a firm who was a respondent to FOS action and who is challenging an award should name the complainant as an interested party; a complainant that is challenging an award should name the firm that was the respondent before the FOS proceedings as an interested party.

Depending on the circumstances, it may also be appropriate to include the FCA as an interested party. This may be appropriate where the FOS decision is said to impinge on or relate to processes instigated by the FCA.[10]

The Claim Form should comply with Part 8 of the CPR, meaning that it should be accompanied by any written evidence that the claimant

---

9 Provision is made for the inclusion of Interested Parties in CPR 54.6(1). There are no specific rules referable to reviews of FOS decisions, but CPR 54APD para 4.6(2) refers to judicial reviews of courts and tribunals, and states that the parties to the decision should be named as interested parties. The same logic applies to judicial review of FOS decisions.

10 As occurred in *R (Full Circle Asset Management Ltd) v FOS* [2017] EWHC 323 (Admin), which raised issues concerning a skilled person's report accepted by the FCA, and in *R (Mazarona Properties Ltd) v FOS* [2017] EWHC 1135 (Admin), relating to a review of interest rate hedging products instigated by the FCA. The FCA has often not appeared as an interested party, despite being named, but it did appear in *Options UK Personal Pensions v FOS* [2024] EWCA Civ 541.

wishes to rely upon.[11] It must then be served within 7 days after the date of issue.[12]

The defendant (i.e. the FOS) and the interested party then have 21 days to file an Acknowledgement of Service,[13] which should include a summary of grounds for contesting the claim. A failure to file an Acknowledgement of Service does not mean that the judicial review will automatically succeed, though a party that fails to file an Acknowledgement will be unable to take part in a hearing as to whether permission for the judicial review should be granted.[14]

The court will then proceed to consider whether permission should be granted for judicial review to proceed. Permission depends on the court being satisfied that there is an arguable case for the claim which has a realistic prospect of success.[15] Normally, the court will reach this conclusion on the papers (i.e. without a hearing). If permission is not given, the claimant can then request an oral hearing to reconsider the matter. There will be such a hearing unless the court concludes that the application is totally without merit.[16]

If the court gives permission for the judicial review, then the defendant (i.e. the FOS) and the interested party may file a detailed Response to the claim, together with any evidence that they wish to rely upon, within 35 days of the order giving permission.[17]

The judicial review will then proceed to a substantive hearing, which is usually conducted using written evidence. It is unusual to have cross-examination of witnesses in a judicial review claim.

---

11 CPR 8.5.

12 CPR 54.7.

13 CPR 54.8.

14 CPR 54.9.

15 *Sharma v Brown-Antoine* [2006] UKPC 87; [2007] 1 WLR 780.

16 CPR 54.12(7).

17 CPR 54.14.

Grounds of challenge

The categories of challenge considered below are not unique to judicial reviews of FOS decisions. They depend on the general principles of judicial review, which are applicable to all bodies whose conduct can be challenged through that process. Nonetheless, we set out below how those principles tend to apply in the context of judicial reviews of the FOS.

It is important to there is no ground for review which provides that the FOS simply 'got the facts wrong'. The courts will not engage with that question, unless it can be shown that the wrongness of the decision falls into one of the following categories.

Jurisdiction

If the FOS did not have jurisdiction to reach the decision that it did, then the court will quash the decision.

There is a particular issue with the three-month time limit for judicial review actions when challenging jurisdiction. This is because the FOS will often resolve the question of its own jurisdiction at an early stage of proceedings (see Chapter 8). If the FOS rules that it does not have jurisdiction, then the complainant will need to commence judicial review proceedings promptly.

What should a respondent to FOS proceedings do, however, where the FOS concludes that it does have jurisdiction, contrary to the respondent's objections? Should it issue a Claim Form immediately, or only after the final decision on the complaint?

In the past, the FOS argued that there was no need to challenge jurisdiction until the final decision has been reached, because it continues to review its own jurisdiction until the final decision on the merits.[18] This argument did not find favour with the courts, and there are numerous judicial review claims on jurisdictional issues determined prior to the

---

18 *R (Chancery (UK) LLP) v FOS* [2015] EWHC 407 (Admin) at [78].

final decision on the merits.[19]

Nevertheless, it may still be possible for a firm unhappy with a jurisdictional decision to await the final decision on the merits before judicially reviewing the FOS. If a firm intends to take this approach, it would be sensible to seek explicit agreement from the FOS that jurisdiction will remain under review and that there is no need to issue a claim for judicial review until after the final decision on the merits.[20]

As to the substance of judicial review claims on jurisdiction, it will be necessary to show that the FOS has stepped outside the limits of its jurisdiction as set out under FSMA or DISP, or alternatively has refused to consider a complaint that it did have jurisdiction over. For details on the FOS's jurisdiction, see Chapters 3 to 6.

The question of jurisdiction is not a question of what is 'fair and reasonable' but a question of law depending on statutory construction. If the FOS has misdirected itself on the law, either as to the legal test or the application of that test, then the court will review the FOS's conclusions.

It has been argued that there are some facts which are 'jurisdictional facts', where the FOS's answer should not be conclusive.[21] This was largely rejected in *R (Assurant General Insurance Ltd) v FOS* [2023] EWCA Civ 1049. The Court of Appeal emphasised at [57] that, in general, questions of fact are for the FOS to determine, subject only to normal public law grounds of judicial review (i.e., irrationality etc). However, the same case at [39]-[45] left open the possibility that there could be hard-edged

---

19 See for example *R (Brinsons) v FOS* [2007] EWHC 2534 (Admin) at [29] and *R (Chancery (UK) Ltd) v FOS* [2015] EWHC 407 (Admin) at [80]. In *R (Assurant General Insurance Ltd) v FOS* [2022] EWHC 2766 (Admin) at [27], Collins Rice J noted that no such argument relating to whether the challenge was made prematurely was pursued by the FOS. At [24] the court emphasised the iterative approach leading to 'final decisions' on jurisdiction.

20 As described in *R (iDealing.com) v FOS* [2024] EWHC 847 (Admin) at [39], albeit noting that this is strictly a matter for the court and not for agreement between the parties.

21 See, for example, *R (Bluefin) v FOS* [2014] EWHC 3431 (Admin) at [41].

'precedent facts', where the court would have to take its own view.

Despite the court's willingness to engage with legal arguments on the FOS's jurisdiction, most attempted judicial reviews on this basis have still failed.

The issue has been raised in the following cases:

1. In *R (Ropaigealach) v FOS* [2005] EWCA Civ 269, it was argued by a complainant that, amongst other things, the FOS had misapplied its own time limits, such that it did have jurisdiction to consider the complaint. The court rejected this argument, as the complaint was clearly out of time.

2. In *R (London Capital Group) v FOS* [2013] EWHC 2425 (Admin), the court considered whether the FOS has jurisdiction in relation to foreign exchange trading accounts. This involved a dispute as to whether such accounts involve investments specified in the RAO. The court concluded that the relevant accounts involved contracts for difference and were therefore within the FOS's jurisdiction. The judicial review therefore failed.

3. In *R (Bluefin Insurance Services Ltd) v FOS* [2014] EWHC 3413 (Admin), the court considered whether a complainant was an eligible complainant (see Chapter 3). This was said to require a hard-edged finding of an objective fact, which the court was required to assess.[22] The court concluded that a director of a business, complaining about the administration of an insurance policy which he claimed should have protected him, was not a consumer. This was because the claim related to his acts as director, forming part of his business or trade.[23] Accordingly, the FOS did not have jurisdiction and the judicial review succeeded.

4. In *R (Chancery (UK) LLP) v FOS* [2015] EWHC 407 (Admin), the question was whether tax advice involving collective

22 At [67].

23 At [116]–[123].

investment schemes fell within the FOS's jurisdiction. The court concluded that tax advice and investment advice were not mutually exclusive: where there was advice on the merits of investments that fell within FSMA, the FOS had jurisdiction.[24]

5. In *R (Mazarona Properties Ltd) v FOS* [2017] EWHC 1135 (Admin), the court decided that the FOS had no jurisdiction to consider complaints arising out of a review of interest rate hedging products, instituted pursuant to an agreement with the FCA. The conduct of such a review is not a 'financial service' for the purpose of the FOS's jurisdiction.

6. In *R (Mortgage Agency Service Number Five) v FOS* [2022] EWHC 1979 (Admin) a firm argued that the FOS's decision to consider matters pre-dating the six-year limitation period (as to which, see Chapter 6) as 'background' to complaints within the limitation period was outside the FOS's jurisdiction. The court disagreed.

7. In *R (Assurant General Insurance Ltd) v FOS* [2023] EWCA Civ 1049, the FOS's jurisdiction depended on whether retailers were to be characterised as agents of an insurance company. On the facts of the case that depended on the construction of contracts, which raised questions of law. The Court of Appeal concluded that the FOS was correct that the retailers were agents, and so had jurisdiction.

8. In *R (Linear Investments Ltd) v FOS* [2024] EWHC 1428 (Admin), it was argued that the complainant was not a consumer and so the FOS did not have jurisdiction. The court agreed with the FOS's analysis, and so it had jurisdiction.

<u>Other mistakes of law</u>

It may also be possible to judicially review a FOS decision based on some mistake of law other than one going to the FOS's jurisdiction. As

[24] At [93-94].

explained in Chapter 11, the FOS is not obliged to follow the law in making its decisions, but it is supposed to take the legal position into account.

R (Shawbrook) v FOS [2023] EWHC 1069 (Admin) ('*Shawbrook*') demonstrates the difference between getting the law wrong, and errors in applying the law. In that case, the court considered a number of alternative bases on which the FOS had found in favour of complainants who had purchased 'fractional ownership timeshares'.

Whilst ultimately the court concluded that the FOS's decisions should be upheld on one particular basis, it also considered a variety of other issues which (in another case) might be crucial. Those issues included areas where the FOS was found to have erred in law and, if those issues had been the only basis for the FOS's approach, the FOS's decisions would have been set aside.[25] In other areas, however, the court was content that the FOS had correctly identified the legal position, even if the court might have disagreed with how those legal principles were applied to the facts of the case (there being no permission in that case to pursue judicial review on the basis of perversity or irrationality).[26]

Similarly, in *R (Critchley) v FOS* [2019] EWHC 3036 (Admin), the court rejected a judicial review of the approach that the FOS had taken to a presumption of inducement in relation to the mis-selling of PPI policies. Having concluded that the FOS had correctly interpreted the rules, the court did not interfere with the FOS's application of those rules.[27]

There remains a difficult question about the extent to which the courts should interfere with the FOS's interpretation of contracts. In *R (TF Global Markets) v FOS* [2020] EWHC 3178 (Admin), the interpretation of contracts was treated as a question of law, such that the court could

---

25 See [54], [121].

26 See [77].

27 See also *R (Berkeley Burke) v FOS* [2018] EWHC 2878 (Admin) at [82]: '*there is an important distinction between (i) construction of the rules (Which is a matter for the court), and (ii) the application of those rules to the facts of the case, which is a matter for the decision-maker.*'

intervene. On the other hand, there are some indications in *Shawbrook* that interpretation of contracts, at least in the context of working out whether the terms are unfair, was an evaluative matter for the FOS rather than a question of law.[28]

Provided the FOS does not get the law wrong, it is not bound to apply the law, and if it takes the view that it is fair and reasonable to depart from the strict legal position, it can only be challenged if the view is perverse or irrational: *R (IFG Financial Services Ltd) v FOS* [2005] EWHC 1153 (Admin). In that case, the fact that the FOS did not apply the rule in *SAAMCO*[29] to the facts of the case did not mean that it was irrational. The reasons for the FOS's departure from the strict legal position were sufficiently clear.

The position appears to be, therefore, that if the FOS correctly identifies the law (or, at least, does not misstate the law) then the decision can only be challenged on irrationality grounds as discussed below, even if the FOS does not apply the law to the facts of the individual complaint. If it misstates the law, then it cannot be said properly to have taken the law into account, and a challenge may succeed.[30]

This is broadly consistent with the approach in *R (Norwich and Peterborough Building Society) v FOS* [2002] EWHC 2379 (Admin). The court considered the FOS's approach to the Banking Code, concluding that if the FOS misconstrued the Code then it failed to take into account a material consideration, such that its decision would be irrational.[31] On the other hand, if the Code was construed properly then the FOS would be given wide leeway in its application of the Code. On the facts of the case, the FOS was found to have misconstrued the Code, but the judicial review failed on the basis that the FOS's decision was supportable for other reasons.

---

28 [2023] EWHC 1069 (Admin) at [168]–[171].

29 *South Australia Asset Management Corp v York Montague* [1997] AC 191.

30 See Collins Rice J's summary in *R (Shawbrook) v FOS* [2023] EWHC 1069 (Admin) at [13].

31 At [79].

Irrationality/Failure to take relevant factors into account

As we have noted above, a judicial review will not succeed because the FOS merely 'got the facts wrong'. Instead, it will be necessary to show that the decision was so wrong that it was irrational. The test is whether the decision was '*so outrageous in its defiance of logic or of accepted moral standards that no sensible person who had applied his mind to the question to be decided could have arrived at it.*'[32]

In this context, the courts have distinguished between findings which rely upon the expertise of the decision maker, and findings where no expertise is needed. It is harder to challenge the former.[33] Nevertheless, it is not enough to argue that the FOS may have got findings of fact wrong: the test is still whether the finding of fact was irrational.

Cases in which irrationality has been pursued as a ground for judicial review include:

1. *R (Garrison Investment Analysis) v FOS* [2006] EWHC 2466 (Admin), which is a rare instance where an irrationality argument succeeded. The challenge was limited to the calculation of quantum. The FOS had accepted that the complainants would have accepted some risk, yet the ombudsman's award proceeded on the basis that they would have accepted none. Sullivan J concluded that this was 'inexplicable' and quashed the decision on this point, indicating the approach that he considered the FOS should take when reconsidering the decision.

2. *R (Green) v FOS* [2012] EWHC 1253 (Admin) was a case in which an IFA argued that the FOS had been wrong to conclude that bad advice had been provided, and that the complainants would have acted differently if other advice had been given. The court noted the risk that the complainant's evidence was unreliable but concluded that the FOS's decision was not

32 *CSSU v Minister of the Civil Service* [1985] AC 374, quoted in *R (Aviva Life and Pensions (UK) Ltd) v FOS* [2017] EWHC 352 (Admin) at [58].

33 *R (Green) v FOS* [2012] EWHC 1253 (Admin) at [11].

irrational. This decision is notable because the court implied that it would have reached a different conclusion if making the decision itself, but it upheld the FOS's decision as rational.

3. In *R (Bankole) v FOS* [2012] EWHC 3555 (Admin) the complainant challenged the FOS's conclusion that he had received the respondent firm's final letter of response, triggering the six-month period in which to pursue a complaint (see Chapter 3). The FOS had provided reasons for its conclusions and could not be overturned as irrational or unsupported by evidence.

4. *R (Walker) v FOS* [2013] NIQB 12 concerned whether the FOS had incorrectly reached conclusions as to the appropriateness of a mortgage. On the facts of the case, where the relevant matters had previously been considered by a court with the same outcome as the FOS, it is not surprising that the court held that the FOS's conclusions were reasonable.

5. In *R (Chancery (UK) LLP) v FOS* [2015] EWHC 407 (Admin), it was argued that the FOS was irrational not to dismiss the complaint as more suitable for determination by a court (see Chapter 16) on the basis that there were a large number of claims with similar issues, involving large sums of money. It was argued that the FOS was an inappropriate forum, but again the court concluded that the FOS was not irrational in concluding otherwise.

6. *R (Kelly) v FOS* [2017] EWHC 3581 (Admin) is another rare case where an irrationality challenge succeeded. The court agreed that the FOS had failed to understand the consumer's complaint and so reached a decision that failed to address it.

7. In *R (Portal Financial Services) v FOS* [2022] EWHC 710 (Admin), it was said that there was no proper argument that the FOS had been irrational in concluding that FSA guidance represented good industry practice, which a pension advisor had breached.

8. In *R (Moniak) v FOS* [2023] EWHC 333 (Admin), the FOS was found to have acted irrationally in refusing to treat evidence obtained by a complainant as 'material new evidence' (see Chapter 8).

9. In *R (Charles Street Securities) v FOS* [2023] EWHC 448 (Admin), the court rejected as 'hopeless' various suggestions that the FOS was irrational in finding that advice had been given or that an advisor was under no duty to consider the losses that a client was able to bear. The court was clearly impressed by the long and detailed FOS decision, and unimpressed by the firm seeking to rerun the same arguments that had lost before the FOS.

10. In *Options UK Personal Pensions v FOS* [2024] EWCA Civ 541, various complaints were made about the FOS's findings of steps that the firm should have taken. They came nowhere near to demonstrating irrationality.

11. In *R (Linear Investments Ltd) v FOS* [2024] EWHC 1428 (Admin), a firm argued that FOS's conclusions on contributory negligence and quantum were irrational. These arguments were given short shrift, and the judicial review failed.

A different way of pursuing the same argument may be to say that the FOS failed to take into account a relevant consideration, or took into account an irrelevant consideration, such that the whole decision can be impeached. This was the position in the *Norwich and Peterborough Building Society* case, described under 'other mistakes of law' above.

Procedural fairness

There are several grounds on which FOS decisions might be challenged by reference to procedural fairness.

Although a concept with a long history, many such challenges would now be pursued by reference to Article 6 of the European Convention on Human Rights. Article 6 states that every person to a dispute is entitled to a fair and public hearing within a reasonable time, conducted by an independent and impartial tribunal. As we explain in Chapter 10, and return to below, this does not generally extend to any right to an oral hearing before the FOS.

The FOS is a tribunal for the purpose of Article 6,[34] and it must act fairly in reaching its decisions.[35] However, the nature of the FOS as a decision-making body means that it is not bound to take the same approach as a court would. For example, a court would not normally consider matters beyond those put forward by the parties. The FOS, on the other hand, is entitled to do so provided the parties have an opportunity to address those matters. This is in part a reflection of the fact that the parties, and complainants in particular, are not usually represented.

An element of the right to a fair hearing is the requirement that a party know the allegations pursued against it. In *R (Bruce) v FOS* [2007] Pens LR 287, a partner in a respondent firm argued that she had not been notified of the complaint prior to the FOS's provisional decision. In consequence, she argued that she had not been able to participate in the investigation of the facts and there had been a breach of natural justice. The court disagreed. First, the firm was on notice as to the complaint even if an individual partner was not.[36] Secondly, the partner failed to put forward any defence to the claim even during the judicial review. Hodge J refused to remit the decision to the FOS where there was no reason for thinking that a different decision would be reached.

It is also important to note that the procedures adopted by the FOS (through investigators, and the use of provisional decisions) will usually mean that by the time the final decision is made, the basis of the complainant is obvious to the respondent.[37] This means that the scope for challenging a FOS decision on the basis that the respondent did not know the case they had to meet is limited.

---

34 *R (Calland) v FOS* [2013] EWHC 1327 (Admin) at [35].

35 *R (Green) v FOS* [2003] EWHC 338 (Admin) at [39].

36 This is now dealt with explicitly by DISP 3.1.3R.

37 *R (Green) v FOS* [2003] EWHC 338 (Admin) at [42]–[52].

It is possible that severe delay by the FOS might constitute a contravention of Article 6 of the European Convention on Human Rights, which refers to decisions being reached within a reasonable time. We are only aware of one case in which this argument was pursued: *R (Calland) v FOS* [2013] EWHC 1327 (Admin). The final decision in that case had taken six years, but the court found that this was largely caused by the attitude of the firm, and that in any event it would not lead to the reversal of the decision absent some unfairness cause by the delay.

In short, there are great difficulties with judicially reviewing the FOS based on the grounds above. However, we are of the view that the court would intervene if a procedure adopted by the FOS was palpably unfair. For example, if a FOS decision relied on key documents, or a witness statement, supplied by one party but not shown or described to the other party, the court might take a dim view of that approach.

R (Kelly) v FOS [2017] EWHC 3581 (Admin) involved slightly different issues, in that the complainant was not upset about the procedural steps *per se*. Instead, it was said that the FOS had misunderstood the nature of the complaint pursued. The court agreed, concluding that the FOS's decision suffered from a procedural error[38] and needed to be retaken.

Bias

There can be no doubt that a FOS decision would be reviewable if there was evidence that the decision was tainted by actual or apparent bias of an ombudsman. There is a long common law history to judicial reviews based on bias, but the case law will now also take into account Article 6 of the European Convention on Human Rights.

To show actual bias, it would be necessary to show that the ombudsman deciding the complaint had a direct personal interest or connection to the matter, or something similar.

Given the difficulties in proving actual bias, parties usually argue that there were facts about the decision maker that give rise to apparent bias.

[38] As characterised by the court at [17].

The test for apparent bias is that the circumstances would lead a fair-minded and informed observer to conclude that there was a real possibility that the decision maker was biased.[39] In cases involving the judiciary, the way in which the judge conducts themselves both inside[40] and outside court[41] may give rise to apparent bias.

Accordingly, there might well be good grounds for challenge if it could be shown that the ombudsman, or possibly the investigator, had a close personal or professional relationship with either the complainant or the respondent firm. Likewise, any animosity shown by the ombudsman or investigator could give rise to apparent bias.

No reported case has featured such facts. It was argued in both *R (Bamber) v FOS* [2009] EWCA Civ 593 and *R (Heather Moor & Edgecomb) v FOS* [2009] EWHC 2701 (Admin) that the relationship between the FOS and the FCA (the FSA, as it then was) demonstrated that the FOS was not independent, but that argument was rejected.[42]

Likewise, *R (Calland) v FOS* [2013] EWHC 1327 (Admin) featured allegations of 'collusion' between the FOS and the FCA (then FSA), but which the court dismissed.[43] The court considered that references from the FSA was a 'somewhat tangled' way for complaints to arise, but held there had been nothing improper in it.[44]

39 *Porter v Magill* [2001] UKHL 67; [2002] 2 AC 357 at [102]–[103].

40 For example, if a judge is openly antagonistic towards a party: *Howell v Millais* [2007] EWCA Civ 720.

41 E.g. in *Locabail v Bayfield Properties* [2000] 2 WLR 870 at [89], a judge's articles in various publications, antagonistic to insurers, was found to give rise to apparent bias.

42 At [16]–[19].

43 See [25].

44 See [21], [55], [57] and [120].

Insufficiency of reasons

A FOS decision should set out sufficient reasons that the parties (and the court) can understand the facts and reasoning which the led the FOS to its result.[45]

The requirement is not as high as it would be for a court. Given the informal nature of FOS complaints, it will be sufficient if the FOS approaches matters on a common sense basis, and it is not required to address every argument put forward by the parties, as long as the conclusion is clear.[46]

This is an area where the courts have been known to find fault with the FOS and, on at least one occasion, remit the decision to the FOS:

1. In *R (Duff) v FOS* [2006] EWHC 1704 at [6] the court concluded that there had 'perhaps' been insufficient reasons given by the FOS on a particular point but agreed with the FOS that the complainant should be left to his alternative remedy of commencing litigation (see below).

2. In *R (Garrison Investment Analysis) v FOS* [2006] EWHC 2466 (Admin), the FOS's approach to quantum calculations was found to be 'inexplicable',[47] and the case was remitted to the FOS. This finding was supported by a conclusion that the FOS's approach had been irrational (see above).

Moreover, there have been cases in which the FOS itself accepted that its decision included insufficient explanation and agreed to reconsider matters without the matter proceeding to judicial review.[48]

Any party challenging a FOS decision on the basis that insufficient

---

45 *R (Young Ridgway) v FOS* [2004] EWHC 3371 (Admin) at [30]–[33].

46 *R (Garrison Investment Analysis) v FOS* [2006] EWHC 2466 (Admin) at [5].

47 At [21].

48 *R (Full Circle Asset Management) v FOS* [2017] EWHC 323 (Admin); *R (Aviva Life and Pensions (UK) Ltd) v FOS* [2017] EWHC 352 (Admin); *Berkeley Burke Sipp Administration v Charlton* [2017] EWHC 2396 (Comm).

reasons were given should remember that the first decision may be overturned, but the FOS will be given an opportunity to reconsider. The FOS may well reach the same conclusion the second time, albeit with fuller reasoning.

Lack of an oral hearing

In Chapter 10, we set out the FOS's approach to oral hearings, and the fact that they are very much the exception rather than the rule. Nonetheless, the lack of an oral hearing is an argument that has often been pursued in judicial review proceedings as a ground for challenging decisions, and the courts have indicated that in appropriate cases an oral hearing might be necessary:

1. In *R (Ropaigealach) v FOS* [2005] EWCA Civ 269, the court stated that there is no entitlement to an oral hearing where the decision-maker is of the view that they have sufficient information.[49] This would suggest that the decision not to hold an oral hearing could only be challenged if the decision-maker irrationally thought that one was unnecessary.

2. In *R (Heather Moor & Edgecomb) v FOS* [2008] EWCA Civ 642, the Court of Appeal gave a more fully reasoned decision, suggesting that if the determination of a complaint involved the resolution of disputes as to what was said at a meeting, then fairness would require an oral hearing.[50] However, it was also suggested that it is not normally necessary for such a hearing, and that the Article 6 right to a public hearing is satisfied by the availability of judicial review proceedings.[51]

3. *R (Heather Moor & Edgecomb) v FOS* [2009] EWHC 2701 (Admin) was a separate judicial review proceeding by the same firm (in relation to a different complaint). HHJ Davis stated that

---

49 At [16].

50 At [58].

51 At [67].

there may be cases in which a public hearing is necessary, but not where there is a comprehensive written record.[52]

4. In *R (Calland) v FOS* [2013] EWHC 1327 (Admin), Males J stated that he considered that it was up to the court – not the FOS – to decide whether fairness requires an oral hearing.[53] This suggests that irrationality is not the test, but again on the facts of the case before him Males J concluded that an oral hearing would have been unlikely to have assisted the FOS and so it was not necessary.

Arbitrariness, or not treating like cases alike

In *R (Heather Moor & Edgecomb) v FOS* [2008] EWCA Civ 642, the Court of Appeal considered another aspect of Convention rights, that FOS decisions could be challenged if they were demonstrably arbitrary: '*Arbitrariness on the part of the ombudsman, including an unreasoned and unjustified failure to treat like cases alike would be a ground for judicial review*'.[54]

However, the court noted the FOS's stated aim of consistency and dismissed the argument.

In *R (Berkeley Burke) v FOS* [2018] EWHC 2878 (Admin), the court also dismissed an argument that the FOS acted in error by failing to follow decisions of the Pensions Ombudsman Service. The two bodies operate under different statutory schemes, and the FOS had reached a conclusion that was not otherwise wrong in law, or perverse. The court gave short shrift to the firm's appeal to consistency.[55]

In practice, it will be difficult to persuade a court that the FOS has acted in an arbitrary way, unless perhaps a FOS decision runs counter to the

52 At [10].

53 At [79].

54 At [49].

55 See [143].

FOS's stated position on a particular issue.

Excessive use of an ombudsman's own knowledge

In judicial proceedings, there are limits on a judge's ability to rely on his/her own knowledge of facts that have not been presented to the court. 'Judicial notice' allows a judge to rely on matters that are common knowledge, but what is the position with the FOS? On the one hand, the FOS is established as a specialist scheme employing ombudsmen with knowledge of the industry. On the other hand, there is a danger of personal bias creeping in if the ombudsman relies on his/her own experience.

R (Williams) v FOS [2008] EWHC 2142 (Admin) suggests that there should be some limit on the use of personal experience, where complaints relate to rare or complicated historical matters.

At the same time, the case also shows the difficulties with judicially reviewing such a decision: it will be necessary to show that the FOS acted irrationally, a difficult test to satisfy.

Relevance of alternative remedies

There are conflicting decisions as to whether judicial review should be refused on the basis that the complainant has an 'alternative remedy'.

In *R (Duff) v FOS* [2006] EWHC 1704 (Admin) it was suggested that a successful judicial review in favour of a complainant would be '*very rare*', on the basis that the complainant would always have the alternative remedy of court proceedings.[56] In general, judicial review will be refused when such alternative remedies exist.

On the other hand, *R (Walker) v FOS* [2013] NIQB 12 reached the opposite conclusion, noting that this approach would force the complainant into court proceedings, which the FOS was set up to avoid.

[56] At [7].

This is a Northern Ireland case, but a similar conclusion was reached by the English court in *R (Fisher) v FOS* (2014, unreported), which is to the effect that judicial review should not be refused because of the existence of alternative remedies.

The remedy in judicial review proceedings

If the judicial review is successful, then the appropriate order will depend on the grounds of the judicial review.

If the FOS has no jurisdiction to consider the compliant, then the FOS's decision will be quashed and that will normally be the end of the FOS complaint.

If the FOS decision suffered from a procedural irregularity or insufficient reasons, then the usual order would be to quash the FOS's decision and to remit the complaint to the FOS to reconsider.

If the question is one of irrationality, then the usual order would be to quash the FOS's decision and remit it for reconsideration, unless there would only be one rational answer. If there is only one rational answer, then the FOS can be directed to reach that answer.[57]

The court has a jurisdiction to quash the entire decision, or just one part of it: in *R (Aviva Life & Pensions (UK) Ltd) v FOS* [2017] EWHC 352 (Admin), a decision was quashed because of inadequate reasons. The firm suggested that the FOS should only reconsider the element of the complaint that the FOS had upheld. On the facts of that case, the entirety of the decision was quashed.

57 *R (Aviva Life and Pensions (UK) Ltd) v FOS* [2017] EWHC 352 (Admin) at [57]. Also see *R (Garrison Investment Analysis) v FOS* [2006] EWHC 2466 (Admin), where the court concluded that the FOS had taken the wrong approach to its calculation of loss, by reference to the Bank of England Base Rate. Concluding that the complainants would have invested in equities, the court commented that the losses should have been calculated by reference to an appropriate index.

Costs of the judicial review

In general, the costs of a judicial review of the FOS will follow the normal principles in such cases: the victor would expect to receive their costs from the losing party.

However, special factors may apply to a judicial review, which may give rise to more unusual cost orders: if the judicial review is pursued by a firm who was a respondent to the FOS proceedings, it is possible that the court may make an order that the firm pay the complainant's costs, irrespective of the outcome. There is only one reported case in which this has happened, where the dispute revolved around the quantum of compensation rather than the validity of the complaint.[58] It is notable that, in that case, the order was made by a judge at first instance, and Laws LJ in the Court of Appeal suggested that he might not have made the same order.

Generally, the FOS will be awarded its costs if it successfully sees off a judicial review. An interested party will not be awarded costs unless it can show that it had a sufficiently good reason for attending in addition to the FOS.[59] In one case, an attempt by a bank, as an interested party, to obtain its costs was given very short shrift.[60]

Refusing to comply with the decision

This chapter has focused on judicial review, and there is no doubt that a judicial review against the FOS is the conventional way to challenge a FOS award.

However, the case of *Bunney v Burns Anderson* [2007] EWHC 1240 (Ch) suggests another avenue that may be available to firms who are respondents to FOS complaints: to refuse to comply with the award and

58 *R (Towry Law Financial Services Ltd) v FOS* [2004] EWCA Civ 1701.

59 *Bolton Metropolitan District Council v Secretary of State for the Environment* [1995] 1 WLR 1176.

60 *R (Mazarona Properties Ltd) v FOS* [2017] EWHC 1135 (Admin).

await enforcement action from the complainant. The judge in that case suggested that firms could resist enforcement without starting a judicial review, at least where the challenge was to the validity of the FOS award, not its merits.[61]

So, if a respondent firm wishes to argue that the FOS exceeded its jurisdiction, then it could leave it to the complainant to start court action. This would require the complainant to pay the court fees and expose the complainant to legal costs. It would also avoid the three-month time period applicable to judicial review claims.

There are some health warnings to such an approach:

1. The FCA might not look kindly on a respondent taking this approach. As noted in the opening paragraph of this chapter, firms have had their authorisation cancelled for failing to comply with FOS decisions. The context of the *Bunney* decision is important in this regard: the firm in that case was willing to comply with the FOS decision up to the financial cap. It was only refusing to comply with the FOS decision to the extent that it was more costly than the cap.

2. The judge in *Bunney v Burns Anderson* recognised that his conclusions might be controversial and stated he would be receptive to an application for permission to appeal.[62] A future judge, or the Court of Appeal, might disagree with his conclusions.

Appeals under the Arbitration Act 1996 are not available

Finally, there is a mode of challenging a FOS decision which has been resoundingly rejected. In *Berkeley Burke Sipp Administration v Charlton* [2017] EWHC 2396 (Comm), it was argued that a FOS decision could be challenged under section 69 of the Arbitration Act 1996. Teare J

61 At paragraphs [50]–[52].

62 At [79].

concluded that the FOS's jurisdiction is not derived from an agreement between the parties, and as such is not a form of arbitration.

CHAPTER EIGHTEEN

THE RESPONDENT'S INSOLVENCY: THE FSCS AND THE THIRD PARTY (RIGHTS AGAINST INSURERS) ACTS

What does the complainant do if they have obtained a monetary award from the FOS, but the respondent firm does not have any money to pay?

Where the respondent is insolvent,[1] a 'protected claimant' can make a claim against the Financial Services Compensation Scheme, which is a creation of Part XV of FSMA.

Most financial services firms will also have indemnity insurance. It may be that some of these policies exclude sums that have been ordered to be paid by the FOS (or other ombudsman). But, for those that do not, the liability embodied by a FOS award may be capable of enforcement against the respondent's insurer.

This question will be governed by the Third Parties (Rights against Insurers) Act 2010. Essentially, the 2010 Act provides that if a relevant person (here, the insolvent respondent) incurs a liability to a third party, that liability can once established be enforced directly against the insurer. A liability can be established either through using the procedure set out in s.2 of the Act (which will generally be the case for FOS awards), obtaining a judgment or decree, or through an enforceable agreement (which will be the case where FOS proceedings have resulted in a settlement agreement).[2]

1 COMP 6.3.1R defines various situations in which a firm is in default.

2 Section 1(4) of the 2010 Act.

CHAPTER NINETEEN

COMPLAINING ABOUT THE FOS

DISP is concerned with complaints about the services of a firm. But what if someone wants to complain about the FOS?

In the first place, it will normally be impossible to seek damages from the FOS in court. The FOS benefits from a statutory immunity, under FSMA Sch 17, para 10, which means that it cannot be held liable in damages unless it has acted in bad faith or in breach of a person's human rights.

Instead, an unhappy participant in a FOS complaint can pursue a complaint to the FOS itself. The FOS's website explains that the complaint will first be considered by a case handler, and can then be referred to a manager, who will provide a response. There are then two further levels of complaint handling: (i) the Customer Complaints team; and (ii) the Independent Assessor.[1]

The initial steps can take place during or within three months of the decision complaint. The Independent Assessor, however, can only consider matters after a case is closed.

The FOS's website makes it clear that the complaints procedures are limited to concerns about the FOS's service, and that the process is not concerned with the merits of any underlying complaints considered by the FOS.[2]

There is little guidance on the FOS website about possible outcomes of complaints, but some light was cast on matters by the case of *R*

---

1 https://www.financial-ombudsman.org.uk/who-we-are/customer-service/service-complaints.

2 *Ibid.*

(iDealing.com) v FOS [2024] EWHC 847 (Admin). In that case, a firm complained about the FOS's conduct of an underlying complaint. The FOS and the Independent Assessor agreed that there had been delays and other issues and offered compensation of £750. The firm sought judicial review of the decision, because it argued it should have been paid compensation reflecting wasted legal costs spent on the underlying complaint.

The court dismissed the judicial review. Indeed, it was suggested that the complaint scheme's decisions were not amenable to judicial review.

Nevertheless, the judgment explains that internal FOS documentation points towards any payment for poor service being paid on a similar basis to awards for distress and inconvenience against firms. It apparently includes a table suggesting that payments can exceed £10,000.

The court seemed to be content with that overall approach, and suggested that it was reasonable for the FOS not to pay the firm's legal costs, given: (i) the FOS's statutory immunity to costs; (ii) the fact that costs arose out of the underlying complaint, which the complaints scheme does not consider; (iii) the fact that respondent's cannot receive their costs against complainants, under DISP 3.7.1R; and (iv) the lack of any reference to the payment of legal costs in the Independent Assessor's terms of reference.

CHAPTER TWENTY

FOS AND THE FCA CONSUMER DUTY

This final chapter explores in brief the FCA's introduction of the consumer duty and its impact on the handling of complaints by the FOS.

In July 2023, the FCA's new consumer duty came into force. The consumer duty sets higher standards of consumer protection in retail financial markets, to which firms must adhere. It comprises a Consumer Principle (Principle 12), which was added to PRIN 2 of the FCA Handbook and obliges a firm to act to deliver '*good outcomes*' for retail customers. The Consumer Principle is supported by three cross-cutting rules and guidance, including PRIN 2A.

In July 2022, the FCA published a policy statement[1] and finalised guidance[2], which made references to the FOS and the obligations a firm will have in handling complaints. Further, the FOS has considered the effect of the consumer duty in several recent publications, speeches and in its 2023/24 Plans and Budget. Although the effect of the consumer duty on the FOS's complaint handling processes is still emerging, the FOS has provided the following commentary and guidance:

- The consumer duty does not apply retrospectively. The FCA is therefore working closely with the FOS to ensure that complaints are judged and assessed by the standards and rules in place at that time.[3]

---

1 FCA Policy Statement on Consumer Duty PS22/9: https://www.fca.org.uk/publication/policy/ps22-9.pdf.

2 FCA Finalised Guidance on the Consumer Duty (FG22/5): https://www.fca.org.uk/publication/finalised-guidance/fg22-5.pdf.

3 See, for example, FOS Blog 'A new Consumer Duty – setting a higher standard of care for consumers' (8 August 2022). Available at: https://www.financial-ombuds

- Both the FOS and the FCA have recognised the requirement for '*good outcomes*' may lend itself to different interpretations on what this means. Both the FCA and FOS will work closely together[4] and with firms to ensure there is a consistent interpretation of requirements under the consumer duty.

- Where complaints considered by the FOS have potential wider implications, the FOS will provide information about its approach through online case study examples and updated guidance for financial businesses.[5]

- The consumer duty will often be an important consideration for the FOS when deciding whether a firm acted fairly and reasonably. Indeed, the consumer duty is underpinned by concerns of fairness and reasonableness – similar to the fair and reasonable standard against which Ombudsman already judge complaints (see Chapter 11).[6]

- The FOS has created sector-specific directorates internally, covering particular areas, such as investments, insurance and banking. These directorates will be '*homes for specialist knowledge*', making it quicker and easier for firms to get answers and insight. The FOS has asked each directorate to consider what approach to sharing information about complaints works best for them and

---

man.org.uk/data-insight/blogs/new-consumer-duty-setting-higher-standard-care-consumers.

4 In particular, through the Wider Implications Framework of which more information can be found at: https://www.fca.org.uk/about/wider-implications-framework.

5 FOS, 'A new Consumer Duty – setting a higher standard of care for consumers' (8 August 2022). Available at: https://www.financial-ombudsman.org.uk/data-insight/blogs/new-consumer-duty-setting-higher-standard-care-consumers.

6 FOS, 'Consumer Duty countdown: how are we preparing?' (13 June 2023). Available at: https://www.financial-ombudsman.org.uk/news/consumer-duty-countdown.

the customers they serve.[7]

Of the complaints considered by the FOS that concern the consumer duty, poor administration and customer service is among the most frequent. In particular, the consumer duty places a strong emphasis on delivering support to meet the needs of vulnerable customers. Complaints in which the consumer duty is relevant often concern firms who have rigid standard processes, which have failed to meet a specific consumer's needs.[8]

7 Ibid.

8 FOS, 'The Consumer Duty one year on: full speech from Abby Thomas' (31 July 2024). Available at: https://www.financial-ombudsman.org.uk/data-insight/insight/consumer-duty-one-year-speech.

INDEX

'The Electronic Communications Code: A Practical Guide – Second Edition' by Kerry Bretherton KC, James Castle, Mark Loveday
'A Practical Guide to the Independent School Standards – September 2023 Edition' by Sarah McKimm
'A Practical Guide to Estate Administration and Crypto Assets' by Richard Marshall
'A Practical Guide to Parental Alienation in Private and Public Law Children Cases' by Sam King QC & Frankie Shama
'Contested Heritage – Removing Art from Land and Historic Buildings' by Richard Harwood QC, Catherine Dobson, David Sawtell
'The Limits of Separate Legal Personality: When Those Running a Company Can Be Held Personally Liable for Losses Caused to Third Parties Outside of the Company' by Dr Mike Wilkinson
'A Practical Guide to Transgender Law' by Robin Moira White & Nicola Newbegin
'A Practical Guide to 'Stranded Spouses' in Family Law' by Mani Singh Basi
'A Practical Guide to Residential Freehold Conveyancing' by Lorraine Richardson
'A Practical Guide to Pensions on Divorce for Lawyers' by Bryan Scant
'A Practical Guide to Challenging Sham Marriage Allegations in Immigration Law' by Priya Solanki
'A Practical Guide to Digital Communications Evidence in Criminal Law' by Sam Willis
'A Practical Guide to Legal Rights in Scotland' by Sarah-Jane Macdonald
'A Practical Guide to New Build Conveyancing' by Paul Sams & Rebecca East
'A Practical Guide to Inherited Wealth on Divorce' by Hayley Trim
'A Practical Guide to Practice Direction 12J and Domestic Abuse in Private Law Children Proceedings' by Rebecca Cross & Malvika Jaganmohan
'A Practical Guide to Confiscation and Restraint' by Narita Bahra QC, John Carl Townsend, David Winch
'A Practical Guide to the Law of Forests in Scotland' by Philip Buchan
'A Practical Guide to Health and Medical Cases in Immigration Law' by Rebecca Chapman & Miranda Butler
'A Practical Guide to Bad Character Evidence for Criminal Practitioners by Aparna Rao
'A Practical Guide to Extradition Law post-Brexit' by Myles Grandison et al
'A Practical Guide to Hoarding and Mental Health for Housing Lawyers' by Rachel Coyle

'Stephens on Contractual Indemnities' by Richard Stephens
'A Practical Guide to the EU Succession Regulation' by Richard Frimston
'A Practical Guide to Solicitor and Client Costs – Second Edition' by Robin Dunne
'Constructive Dismissal – Practice Pointers and Principles' by Benjimin Burgher
'A Practical Guide to Religion and Belief Discrimination Claims in the Workplace' by Kashif Ali
'A Practical Guide to the Law of Medical Treatment Decisions' by Ben Troke
'Fundamental Dishonesty and QOCS in Personal Injury Proceedings: Law and Practice' by Jake Rowley
'A Practical Guide to the Law in Relation to School Exclusions' by Charlotte Hadfield & Alice de Coverley
'A Practical Guide to Divorce for the Silver Separators' by Karin Walker
'The Right to be Forgotten – The Law and Practical Issues' by Melissa Stock
'A Practical Guide to Planning Law and Rights of Way in National Parks, the Broads and AONBs' by James Maurici QC, James Neill et al
'A Practical Guide to Election Law' by Tom Tabori
'A Practical Guide to the Law in Relation to Surrogacy' by Andrew Powell
'A Practical Guide to Claims Arising from Fatal Accidents – Second Edition' by James Patience
'A Practical Guide to Asbestos Claims' by Jonathan Owen & Gareth McAloon
'A Practical Guide to Stamp Duty Land Tax in England and Northern Ireland' by Suzanne O'Hara
'A Practical Guide to the Law of Farming Partnerships' by Philip Whitcomb
'A Practical Guide to the Law of Unlawful Eviction and Harassment – Second Edition' by Stephanie Lovegrove
'A Practical Guide to Costs in Personal Injury Claims – Second Edition' by Matthew Hoe
'A Practical Guide to the General Data Protection Regulation (GDPR) – Second Edition' by Keith Markham
'A Practical Guide to Working with Litigants in Person and McKenzie Friends in Family Cases' by Stuart Barlow
'Protecting Unregistered Brands: A Practical Guide to the Law of Passing Off' by Lorna Brazell
'A Practical Guide to Secondary Liability and Joint Enterprise Post-Jogee' by Joanne Cecil & James Mehigan

'A Practical Guide to the Pre-Action RTA Claims Protocol for Personal Injury Lawyers' by Antonia Ford
'A Practical Guide to Neighbour Disputes and the Law' by Alexander Walsh
'A Practical Guide to Coercive Control for Legal Practitioners and Victims' by Rachel Horman
'A Practical Guide to the Law of Driverless Cars – Second Edition'
by Alex Glassbrook, Emma Northey & Scarlett Milligan
'A Practical Guide to TOLATA Claims' by Greg Williams
'A Practical Guide to Elderly Law – Second Edition' by Justin Patten
'A Practical Guide to Responding to Housing Disrepair and Unfitness Claims' by Iain Wightwick
'A Practical Guide to the Law of Bullying and Harassment in the Workplace' by Philip Hyland
'How to Be a Freelance Solicitor: A Practical Guide to the SRA-Regulated Freelance Solicitor Model' by Paul Bennett
'A Practical Guide to Prison Injury Claims' by Malcolm Johnson
'A Practical Guide to Advising Clients at the Police Station' by Colin Stephen McKeown-Beaumont
'A Practical Guide to Antisocial Behaviour Injunctions – Second Edition' by Iain Wightwick
'Practical Mediation: A Guide for Mediators, Advocates, Advisers, Lawyers, and Students in Civil, Commercial, Business, Property, Workplace, and Employment Cases' by Jonathan Dingle with John Sephton
'The Mini-Pupillage Workbook' by David Boyle
'A Practical Guide to Crofting Law' by Brian Inkster
'A Practical Guide to the Law of Domain Names and Cybersquatting' by Andrew Clemson
'A Practical Guide to the Law of Gender Pay Gap Reporting' by Harini Iyengar
'NHS Whistleblowing and the Law' by Joseph England
'Employment Law and the Gig Economy' by Nigel Mackay & Annie Powell
'A Practical Guide to Noise Induced Hearing Loss (NIHL) Claims' by Andrew Mckie, Ian Skeate, Gareth McAloon
'An Introduction to Beauty Negligence Claims – A Practical Guide for the Personal Injury Practitioner' by Greg Almond
'Intercompany Agreements for Transfer Pricing Compliance' by Paul Sutton
'Zen and the Art of Mediation' by Martin Plowman
'A Practical Guide to Adoption for Family Lawyers' by Graham Pegg

'A Practical Guide to Industrial Disease Claims' by Andrew Mckie & Ian Skeate
'A Practical Guide to Conducting a Sheriff Court Proof' by Andrew Stevenson
'A Practical Guide to Vicarious Liability' by Mariel Irvine
'A Practical Guide to Applications for Landlord's Consent and Variation of Leases' by Mark Shelton
'A Practical Guide to Relief from Sanctions Post-Mitchell and Denton' by Peter Causton
'A Practical Guide to Equity Release for Advisors' by Paul Sams
'A Practical Guide to Financial Services Claims' by Chris Hegarty
'A Practical Guide to Financial Ombudsman Service Claims' by Adam Temple & Robert Scrivenor
'A Practical Guide to Running Housing Disrepair and Cavity Wall Claims – Second Edition' by Andrew Mckie & Ian Skeate
'A Practical Guide to Holiday Sickness Claims – Second Edition' by Andrew Mckie & Ian Skeate
'Arguments and Tactics for Personal Injury and Clinical Negligence Claims' by Dorian Williams
'A Practical Guide to Drone Law' by Rufus Ballaster, Andrew Firman, Eleanor Clot
'On Experts: CPR35 for Lawyers and Experts' by David Boyle
'An Introduction to Personal Injury Law' by David Boyle

These books and more are available to order online direct from the publisher at www.lawbriefpublishing.com, where you can also read free sample chapters. For any queries, call us on 0844 587 2383 or email us at mail@lawbriefpublishing.com.

Our books are all generally in stock at www.amazon.co.uk with free next day delivery for Prime members, and at good legal bookshops such as Wildy & Sons.

We are regularly launching new books in our series of practical day-to-day practitioners' guides. Visit our website and join our free newsletter to be kept informed and to receive special offers, free chapters, etc.

You can also follow us on Twitter at www.twitter.com/lawbriefpub.

www.ingramcontent.com/pod-product-compliance
Ingram Content Group UK Ltd.
Pitfield, Milton Keynes, MK11 3LW, UK
UKHW020143290926
15471UKWH00004B/678

9 781916 698840